SOARING BEYOND MIDLIFE

The Surprisingly Natural Emergence of
Leadership Superpowers in
Life's Second Half

by
Aneace Haddad

Table Of Contents

Introduction

What if the moment you think everything is ending is actually the beginning?

At 47, the life I had carefully built began to unravel. After finalizing my divorce and selling the tech company I had nurtured in the south of France — a place I called home for twenty years and where I imagined spending my future — I found myself at a crossroads. With my past behind me, I moved to Singapore, poised for new entrepreneurial adventures. Life had other plans.

Though my career had always revolved around technology, it was during this transformative period of midlife that I discovered a surprising truth: I liked people more than computers. The success of former colleagues, who rose to become CEOs, CTOs, and CFOs, brought me immense satisfaction and pride.

This revelation gradually steered me towards executive coaching, where I have since guided many leaders through their own midlife transformations. Drawing on these experiences, this book explores midlife as a profound opportunity for renewal and growth.

Reflecting on my own journey, I recognize it mirrors the experiences of many executives, marked by pivotal changes. Through coaching, I've identified consistent patterns that not only highlight the common challenges of midlife but also its vast opportunities for personal and professional rejuvenation. Inspired by these insights, I wrote this book.

Rather than offering prescriptive steps, this book presents stories and insights that encourage you to explore midlife's unique challenges and opportunities. Welcome to a journey of discovery, where we harness midlife's winds of change to uncover our true strengths and rejuvenate our approach to leadership.

Join me in redefining midlife leadership, as we reevaluate our methods, discard outdated practices, and adopt strategies that enrich the latter half of our careers.

Welcome to the Crucible of Midlife Leadership

Midlife challenges seasoned leaders to reassess their lives and leadership styles. It's a time when the interplay of physiological, neurological, and parental changes prompts us to let go of outdated practices and adapt to new realities.

This period brims with complexity, offering both challenges and exhilarating opportunities for growth that can redefine our personal and professional lives.

Let's look at the Three Winds of Change:

- **The Physiological Wind of Change** heralds a time of physical changes that can deepen our self-understanding and inspire new leadership approaches. Realizing that we're likely only halfway through our careers, we can tap into a renewed energy that defies any ideas of slowing down.
- **The Neurological Wind of Change** unlocks new ways of thinking. During midlife, the brain undergoes subtle changes, potentially affecting cognitive processing and working memory. This period also sees potential for enhanced bilateral collaboration between brain hemispheres, fostering a more integrative and holistic thinking. We might sometimes struggle to recall someone's name or the exact figures in a report, but we're often able to connect the dots in a far more creative manner.
- **The Parental Wind of Change** reflects the evolution in our personal lives, deeply influencing our leadership style. As our children mature from teenagers to young adults, our parenting evolves from daily guidance to supportive empowerment. This change in parenting style is reflected in our approach to leadership, where we move from a directive style to an inspirational style.

We face a pivotal choice: continue with the demanding pace of our youth or lean into the Winds of Change, harnessing the full depth of our experience. This crucial choice lies at the heart of the midlife crucible.

If you're seeking a guide that transcends traditional 'how-to' manuals, offering leadership narratives, practical tools, and personal reflection to inspire and engage you in your midlife journey, this book is written for you.

As you turn these pages, reflect on how these winds of change have been shaping your journey. Are you ready to redefine what it means to be a leader in the prime of your life?

A Perfect Storm for Developing Exceptional Leaders

Soaring Beyond Midlife addresses a crucial gap in leadership literature, which often fails to differentiate between early adulthood and midlife. Despite leadership's pervasive presence online, generating billions of discussions, the critical phase of midlife is often overlooked in leadership studies. This oversight reveals a gap in our understanding of midlife's unique challenges and the lack of tailored development programs for midlife executives.

Some of today's most influential leadership theories date back to three decades ago when social psychologists deemed midlife the 'last uncharted territory in human development.' Although robust and frequently cited in my own work, these theories often overlook the distinct qualities emerging after forty, perpetuating the myth that exceptional leadership traits are rare or innate.

For example, Robert Kegan, an adult-development psychologist, suggests that only about 1% of adults achieve what he calls the self-transforming mind, the highest level in his model. Similarly, Jim Collins, known for 'Good to Great,' describes Level 5 leadership, as the pinnacle of his model, combining humility with fierce resolve. According to Collins, this level of leadership is rare but can be developed under the right circumstances. He suggests these circumstances might include self-reflection, conscious personal development, a mentor, a great teacher, loving parents, or a significant life experience.

This idea forms the core premise of this book. It posits that the right circumstances for such development are inherent in midlife. Furthermore, these opportunities are far more common than we might have previously thought.

While they have greatly advanced our understanding of leadership, prominent figures like Jim Collins, Robert Kegan, Patrick Lencioni, and Simon Sinek all developed their foundational leadership theories before experiencing midlife, typically in their thirties.

While their theories and writings are excellent, the unique phase of midlife, with its distinct challenges and opportunities for growth, remains less examined. This observation extends to writers like Brené Brown, Richard Barrett, Stephen Covey, Marshall Goldsmith, and John Maxwell, whose seminal works, even if published later in their careers, did not explicitly navigate the specific dynamics of midlife leadership. This isn't to detract from their contributions but to highlight an area ripe for further exploration, suggesting that the journey of understanding leadership, especially through the lens of midlife, is an ongoing process.

When I decided to focus exclusively on leaders and C-suite teams over 40, I quickly discovered that it is surprisingly easier to transform top teams when embracing the profound changes inherent in midlife.

Traditional leadership programs tend to be more prescriptive, often designed for executives in the earlier stages of their careers. These programs emphasize skill acquisition and structured learning paths, catering to those still climbing the corporate ladder.

In contrast, leadership development for midlife executives benefits from a fundamentally different approach. At this stage, leaders are often experiencing significant personal and professional transformations, characterized by deeper self-awareness and a reevaluation of their goals and values.

Focusing only on midlife leaders leverages this unique mindset, emphasizing reflective practices, legacy-building, and the integration of personal and professional growth. These programs are less about prescribing a one-size-fits-all path and more about harnessing the rich, introspective energy of midlife to unlock profound, lasting change.

What's been truly surprising to me is how much easier this focus has made my work. The transformations I witness feel more organic and natural, leveraging the profound changes midlife executives are already experiencing. Tapping into these inherent shifts enables the natural emergence of the team's collective best self. This book aims to capture these organic transformations through fiction and poetry, bringing the principles to life in a uniquely engaging way.

Considering the unique perspectives and maturity midlife brings, could it not be a crucible for refining and enhancing leadership qualities often considered rare in younger leaders? What if traits that appear as inherent gifts in younger executives become more prevalent as we age? With a deeper understanding of neuroplasticity and the unique insights offered by midlife, this period presents a prime opportunity to broaden our approach to leadership development.

The Mastery Journey Through CEOs' Eyes

Each chapter of this book narrates a CEO's story. Consider Rajiv, a textile factory CEO in India, grappling with factory accidents. Despite his staunch commitment to 'Safety First', Rajiv found that accidents still occurred. The turning point came when he realized his efforts were at a nine out of ten in commitment. True transformation began only after he deeply understood what a full, ten out of ten commitment to safety entailed — leading to a significant and impactful change in the factory's safety culture.

Nicole, a frustrated interim CEO of a fashion conglomerate in New York City, grapples with a pressing question: Why is the board hesitating to confirm her in the permanent role?

Joanna, at the helm of a pharmaceutical company in Barcelona, realizes her straightforward, no-frills leadership style is pushing her team away.

Then there's Tomas, the CEO of a European cybersecurity firm, wrestling with personal turmoil as his daughter prepares to leave home — a change that mirrors his own intensifying desire for control at work.

Six Midlife Leadership Superpowers

The interplay of physiological, neurological, and parental shifts at midlife – the Three Winds of Change – serves as a powerful catalyst for developing six key leadership superpowers.

Humility and Iron Will: In midlife, seasoned leaders blend unwavering determination with the humility learned from life's transitions. As youth fades and family dynamics evolve, a deeper self-awareness fosters resilience and empathy. This balance of resolve and humility cultivates an adaptable leadership style, deeply attuned to life's complexities.

Continual Rebirth: Midlife leaders have worked in roles from entry-level to executive positions and have gone through major life changes. They understand that people's identities change over time. This understanding makes it easier for them to adapt and reinvent themselves in both their personal lives and their careers.

Boundless Ideation: Midlife sparks a unique blend of analytical and creative thinking. Enhanced integration between brain hemispheres helps leaders transcend conventional boundaries, encouraging innovation within and across teams. This shift transforms challenges into opportunities for visionary and cooperative leadership.

Total Ownership: Deeper hemispheric integration in the brain enhances leaders' grasp of interconnected roles, prompting a shift towards holistic engagement. This insight allows leaders to recognize and inspire their team's full potential, fostering a collective drive towards success.

Timeless Impact: The midlife paradox — feeling time's urgency while recognizing a potentially longer, impactful future — balances immediate actions with long-term planning, deeply shaping leadership identities.

Life Synergy: Midlife often shifts leaders' focus from traditional motivators to a profound appreciation for human connections. This shift encourages a harmonious blend of personal and professional life, moving away from high-stress tasks towards a more rewarding and balanced leadership approach.

Drawing on my previous novel, *The Eagle That Drank Hummingbird Nectar*, this book merges leadership insights with stories, fiction, and poetry. This unique combination, intentional in its design, brings principles to life, evokes emotions, and captivates leaders in a way traditional guides do not. This book is not just a guide — it's an immersive journey into mature leadership.

A Thank You and Invitation

My hope with 'Soaring Beyond Midlife' is to offer you more than just guidance; it's an invitation to embark on a journey of reflection and personal growth. Eschewing the traditional how-to format — which often caters more to budding leaders — I've opted for a deeper exploration of midlife's rich complexities. Through a blend of stories, insights, and exercises, this book is designed to help you unlock your inherent wisdom, which I believe holds the keys to even the most daunting leadership challenges.

For additional tools, resources, and ongoing discussions about transformative leadership, please visit www.aneace.com.

The Author

Aneace Haddad's journey spans four decades and as many continents. His career began in programming in Denver, Colorado, evolved into launching a tech startup in France, and culminated in his role as a C-Suite Coach in Singapore. Working with firms like McKinsey and Deloitte University, Aneace specializes in developing leadership strategies for executives, particularly during the challenging yet transformative midlife period. His global experience and focus on practical strategies make him a valued guide for senior leaders navigating both professional and personal complexities of midlife.

Chapter One
The Seasoned Executive's New Horizon

"But the stress
in my chest, the
restless nights, and
frayed connections, are
warnings I must heed.

My fuel is almost spent, I know,
my way will not propel me further.

With nothing to grasp for safety,
no knowledge, authority, or expertise;
I linger in the black stillness, suspended,
between ascent and descent.

In that stillness, a spark of insight —
I am alive; and I still have dreams."

— **Rajiv Mehta**

Ripples of Authenticity at Lake Como

The conference by Lake Como was in full swing. On the veranda, the cocktail event buzzing with activity, a large digital screen displayed the CEO forum's theme for the year: "Bridging Boundaries: Charting the Course of High-Performing Teams". Below it, an animated banner flashed, proclaiming, "The Key Metrics of Leadership Success!"

At the outskirts of this vibrant scene, four CEOs formed a tense huddle at the lake's edge, their voices subdued under the crisp evening air scented with pine and freshwater.

Joanna Vega said, "Does anyone else feel like we're just echoing what's been said a thousand times before? I mean, strategies, metrics—it's important, but it feels hollow." Her voice was firm yet tinged with frustration.

Rajiv Mehta, always the pragmatist and with his usual analytical tone, countered, "I get where you're coming from, Joanna. It's what people expect, though—concrete strategies, clear metrics. It's comfortable."

Joanna, more to herself than the group, mused, "Maybe comfort isn't what we need right now. How about we dive into what's really transformed us? Rajiv, you've shifted gears dramatically, haven't you?"

Tomas Ferreira and Nicole Parker listened, their gazes ping-ponging between Joanna and Rajiv.

Rajiv, with a half-smile, admitted, "True, there's a lot behind the scenes. Mixing personal growth with our strategies... Could make for a more balanced discussion."

Joanna crossed her arms and shook her head, her gaze reflecting the determination in her voice.

Rajiv turned to Tomas and Nicole. "Tomas, Nicole, what's your take on this?"

Nicole, nodded at Rajiv, "I also think it's those personal breakthroughs that often lead to the most profound changes, in us and our leadership."

Tomas smiled warmly and said, "Hearing about someone's personal evolution—like yours, Rajiv—strikes a deeper chord. It's compelling, real."

Nicole nodded. "Exactly."

Rajiv still looked unconvinced. "I will absolutely not read a poem in front of all these people," he said.

A young attendee stumbled over, slightly tipsy, clutching a champagne glass. His footing was shaky, and his words lightly slurred. "You see that swan over there? The... the older one? They call him Alarico, I think. He's like... I don't know, some wise old bird. Other birds just gather around him. Soakin' up... wisdom, or whatever."

Several water birds floated around the old swan, seemingly listening to it.

Nicole smirked, "Looks like another conference is in session there."

Tomas chuckled, "To be heard without saying a word, now that's something. If only people paid attention to me that way."

Rajiv and Joanna laughed along.

The young man's eyes widened as he recognized them. "Oh, you guys are the keynote speakers, right? Really excited to hear your secret tips!"

Rajiv replied warmly, "You know, the biggest secrets you'll find are often not secrets at all. Sometimes, they're simpler and more profound than we expect."

After the young man left, Joanna smiled at Rajiv, "Rajiv, are you with us on this? Ready to share something unexpected, something real?"

Rajiv, uneasy, said, "I hear what you're all saying. And you're right. In my factory, personal stories made all the difference. It's just..." He glanced over his shoulder, then drew closer to his friends, "With these analysts from Wolf & Mare around, I'm a bit wary. Getting too personal might not sit well with everyone."

Suddenly, the tranquillity was broken as a stone splashed into the lake, startling the birds who took flight. Alarico the swan, however, remained, and his posture one of dignified defiance.

Joanna's face reddened with anger, her voice rising. "What the hell was that for?"

The young attendee shrugged, an uneasy smile on his face.

"Just wanted a closer look at the famous old bird." He glanced at his empty glass and ambled back to the party.

Nicole couldn't hide her disbelief. "Seriously?"

Tomas let out a quiet chuckle.

Nicole turned to him; her eyebrows raised. "What's funny?"

Tomas, chuckling softly, said, "Not the stone-throwing, of course. But it's kind of metaphorical, isn't it? That stone is like my old ways of doing things – splashy, loud. But look at Alarico, unflustered. That's the kind of presence we should aim for – composed, with a quiet depth. Like Lake Como, calm on the surface but with so much mystery underneath."

Rajiv nodded, looking at the swan, "A lesson in grace and strength, from a bird."

A faint cheer erupted from the main event, creating a contrast with their discussion.

Tomas, as he was leaning forward; his eyes bright with conviction, said, "We'd be missing out if we didn't share these insights, these life lessons. Let's show them what leadership really means beyond the buzzwords."

Nicole gave a double thumbs-up.

Rajiv stared at his palms as if searching for a clue. Then he slowly nodded. "Being vulnerable got us here. If my team can handle seeing me vulnerable, so can they."

Tomas put his hand on Rajiv's shoulder and added, "Your vulnerability has saved lives, my friend. Let's show them real leadership isn't about the noise you make, but the depth you bring from living a full life. Authenticity, not just showmanship."

As they returned to the main event, a sense of camaraderie and purpose united them. They were no longer just individual leaders from different corners of the globe but a collective voice, ready to speak on the profound and often overlooked aspects of leadership transformation at midlife.

As the group relaxed, Tomas, with a light-hearted gesture towards his glass, remarked, "Liquor is the nectar of the gods."

Rajiv, with a playful yet thoughtful smile, corrected, "I think you mean honey."

Tomas laughed, "Right, honey for the soul, liquor for the spirits."

Echoes of Past Journeys

The sentiments shared on that evening by Lake Como were reflections of inner struggles, pivotal moments, and profound realizations. These discussions raised a crucial question: could midlife be a catalyst for transformative growth in both life and career?

One such story was Rajiv's, who learned that the difference between being nearly committed and fully-committed can dramatically alter an organization's path. His journey exemplifies the potential of midlife, often seen as a crisis period, to be a time of significant professional revival and personal awakening.

Let's rewind to a year before the Lake Como conference, a time when the four CEOs had not yet met.

When Nine out of Ten is Mediocre

Rajiv, the CEO of a factory plagued by a series of accidents, was at his wits' end. On the walls of the entry hall hung the company's safety mantra: 'Safety is Job Number One.' Yet, despite significant investments in protocols, consultants, and town hall speeches, the accidents continued. He rated his own commitment to safety a nine-out-of-ten. As his coach, I suggested his not-quite-total commitment might be contributing to these tragedies.

Rajiv bristled. "That's impossible! You don't understand... workers do crazy things! Most of them aren't educated! There are more than two thousand people here... I can't be on their backs every moment!"

And with those words, the 'Secret Saboteur' — the limiting belief hindering him from reaching ten-out-of-ten commitment — began to reveal itself.

He continued, sounding almost like he was ranting. "If somebody needs to get to the other end of the factory," he said in his deep voice, "they'll jump on a forklift going by. They know they're not supposed to, but they do it anyway. They should be able to take care of themselves. They're adults! Not children! I can't be standing behind every single person... to make sure they don't do stupid things!"

"I... I agree."

"So, what the hell are you talking about?"

I wanted to ask if ten-out-of-ten commitment meant supervising every worker, but he was visibly angry and red in the face.

Rajiv became distant, lost in thought, wrestling with profound questions I had never had to face. I felt guilty and powerless. In that moment, I realized my emotions mirrored Rajiv's, a profound moment of empathic resonance experienced by every coach. It felt like stepping into Rajiv's shoes, feeling the weight of his dilemmas. It was a visceral reminder of the human connection at the heart of coaching. Tapping into these emotions, I then noticed the bags under his eyes, his subtle swaying, and sagging shoulders. Rajiv was exhausted. Something I hadn't noticed before caught my eye — Rajiv kept glancing at a picture of his family on his desk; Rajiv, his wife and his son, who looked to be around ten in the picture, all three of them smiling. I knew his son was in his last year of high school, so the picture wasn't recent.

Does ten out of ten commitment really mean being on every worker's back? I wanted so much to ask that question. Realizing the depth of Rajiv's introspection, I decided not to press further. "It seems we've uncovered some significant thoughts today," I remarked gently. "Let's take some time to reflect and revisit these insights in our next session."

Rajiv nodded silently, the weight of the conversation hanging between us.

As our session ended, he accompanied me to the lobby. In the elevator, the silence was palpable. I didn't want to break the quiet ambience, as it would interrupt his contemplation. Rajiv stared at the floor numbers going by on the small screen.

Finally, he spoke softly, "You know, these accidents... they haunt me. It's lives we're talking about. And the families left behind." He shook his head, his voice faltering. His eyes briefly glistened before he composed himself, clearing his throat awkwardly. He seemed embarrassed, and then he looked at me. "I'm still thinking about your question," he said quietly, with a look of vulnerability. "Maybe ten-out-of-ten commitment isn't what I thought it was."

I hadn't actually asked him that, but yeah, he had definitely heard my question.

"You look tired," I said gently. "I hope you're getting enough sleep."

He smiled wryly, It was the kind of smile that spoke more of resignation than amusement. "I've never slept much," he said. "Four or five hours a night. It's always worked for me."

I nodded, noticing his sigh. He knew he needed more sleep.

"Well," he continued, "It always worked for me before."

"Our bodies change," I said. "It's sometimes hard to deal with."

He nodded.

An early morning call

My phone vibrated with a text message at 7am. It was Rajiv. "Can I call you now?" He asked. It was only 4:30am in Mumbai, so I got concerned and immediately dialed his number.

He let out a heavy sigh, his voice tinged with exhaustion. "I couldn't sleep... there was another incident at the factory last evening. Not fatal, thankfully, but it's shaken me up. I keep thinking about what we discussed regarding safety and commitment."

He paused on the other end of the line, and I could almost hear the wheels turning in his mind. Then, almost in a whisper, he added, "What if this is all my fault? I'm failing at work, and at home."

The vulnerability in his voice was striking. I remembered the family picture in Rajiv's office. I prodded, "What's happening at home?"

Slowly exhaling, as if bracing himself to share something deeply personal, Rajiv shared, "It's my son... he doesn't listen to me anymore. He's always out with his friends, and I have no clue what they're up to. I'm so used to having control at work, but with him, I feel helpless. I've tried being strict, but it's only made things worse with my wife."

As Rajiv continued, it became clear to me that the stress of work and the turmoil at home were intersecting and making each other worse. His situation echoed the classic hallmarks of a midlife crisis, where the tangled web of personal and professional challenges demands reevaluation and thoughtful navigation.

Rajiv paused, and I could hear his breath heavy on the other end of the line. "And there's more..." he hesitated. "I've been feeling worn out lately, more than usual. I wake up tired. I can't seem to shake off this fatigue."

His voice dropped to a near whisper, "My father passed away at 67, you know. Heart attack. I'm 45 now, and it hits me... maybe I don't have as much time as I thought. That's scary to think about." A silence fell over Rajiv's side of the line, perhaps a moment for reflection or a sigh too soft for the phone to catch. Then, with a slight shift in his tone, he moved on. "And about the accident at the factory... when I heard about the young man who got injured, I felt this lump in my throat. I have to keep a stern face, no matter what, so that people don't get scared. But now, I get emotional over these things. I can't help it."

I ventured, "You're going through a lot."

He sighed again, "And there's my son. He's growing up, becoming more independent, and we're drifting apart. I don't know how to bridge that gap. It's like I'm losing my grip on things that I used to control so effortlessly."

As he spoke, I saw in Rajiv's narrative the elements of what I later described as the 'Three Winds of Change,' a concept that encapsulates these types of transformations. I wanted to say, Rajiv, what you're experiencing is not uncommon at this stage in life. It's a time of transformation and a powerful opportunity for growth.

Rajiv's voice started regaining a firm tone when he suddenly cut me off, "Navel gazing never solves problems. I need to focus on solutions." It's as if he was eager to rebuild the walls that had momentarily crumbled.

"I understand, Rajiv," I responded, recognizing the need to respect his boundaries. "Focusing on solutions is key."

He cleared his throat, "Yes, well, let's schedule a meeting to discuss action plans for the factory. I'll have my assistant reach out."

The conversation ended. Rajiv was battling not just challenges at his workplace, but also internal conflicts being triggered by subtly profound shifts.

Rajiv's Pivotal Moment:
From Compliance to Compassion

When we met again several weeks later, Rajiv stood tall with a big smile. He closed the conference room door quickly and excitedly, as if eager to start our session. I noticed that the huge banner in the lobby had been changed. Instead of 'Safety is Job Number One', it now said, '10/10 Safety Commitment, Everyone, Everywhere.'

"I've been doing a lot of thinking," Rajiv reflected in an assertive tone. "About everything – safety, leadership, my family, my health. It's all interconnected, isn't it?"

I nodded. "That's definitely the sense I had."

Rajiv leaned forward slightly, hands clasped together as if gathering his thoughts. "A few days after we last talked, something happened that, well, it took me by surprise. I was walking through the factory—" he paused, gesturing with his hands as if walking through the space, "—when I stumbled upon one of our janitors. Poor guy had hurt himself. Nothing too serious, but still, he needed help. So, I called up our medical team right away and stayed with him until they arrived." Rajiv's hands opened in a gesture of care and concern. "That was my nine out of ten. That's what I would normally do."

He leaned back this time and his eyes were filled with self-reflection. "So, the medics checked him over and said he was alright, just needed some rest. And then, before I knew it," he leaned forward again, eyes wide with a hint of surprise, "I found myself offering to drive him home. I've never done anything like that before. It was... different, you know?"

Rajiv's hands mimicked holding a steering wheel. "There I was, driving this guy home, and I ended up meeting his family." He shook his head in disbelief as he chuckled softly. "We had tea, and we talked. I made sure he promised to take it easy before coming back to work."

Rajiv sat back in his seat, staring into the distant with introspection. "You know, I've always been about the big picture, the grand strategy, but this... this was something else. It was personal, real. I guess it showed me a different side of leadership, something more hands-on and, well, human. It felt good, actually, being there for someone like that. It's not something I would have done before, but, well, now..." He spread his hands, a gesture of openness and revelation. "What do you think of that?"

"I think that sounds like ten-out-of-ten commitment," I said.

"Damn right!" Rajiv boomed. "That was my 100 percent. It's like I suddenly saw him not just as an employee, but as a person. And it made me realize, that's what ten out of ten commitment is – it's about seeing people, truly seeing them."

"I noticed the new banner in the lobby," I said.

Rajiv beamed. "Ten-out-of-Ten Safety Commitment, Everyone, Everywhere. That came out of a brainstorming session with my team."

He shared details about the session, which was more than a typical meeting. He had created a space for an open discussion on enterprise-wide commitment to safety, where each person would assume total ownership of their own safety and everyone else's. Each of his direct reports took turns to share what their own personal full commitment would look like, and how it would change their day-to-day operations. Some stumbled over their words, not yet fully grasping the concept. But Rajiv gave them room to grapple with the new idea, just as he had done earlier with his own transition to ten-out-of-ten commitment.

During that brainstorming meeting, the head of HR raised a concern. She suggested that the forced ranking performance system might imply that achieving a perfect score was unattainable. By its very nature, this system compelled managers to classify a certain percentage of employees in the lower ranks, even if their performance was stellar. She had attempted to change the system in the past, but the rest of the team at the top ranks had been resistant, who favored the competitive pressure it fostered.

With a newfound spirit that was already beginning to take shape in the organization, Rajiv and his leadership team resolved to reassess the performance evaluation system, aiming to better reflect their evolving culture.

Rajiv placed his hands firmly on the conference table. "The

culture is shifting," he said. "I can sense it. We haven't had a single incident in two weeks. No changes in safety procedures, just a different way of being, starting with me. At nine-out-of-ten, we still blame the world and want to change others. At ten-out-of-ten, we roll up our sleeves and change ourselves."

He then shared a thought that struck a chord with me: "It's funny how age changes your perspective. In my thirties, I was all about the hustle, being the toughest and the smartest guy in the room. But now, at 45, I find myself asking different questions, looking for deeper meaning. It's not just about the what, but the how and the why."

This pivot in Rajiv's understanding mirrors a larger societal shift in how we approach midlife. No longer is this period just a marker of age; it's increasingly seen as an opportunity for profound personal and professional transformation. Rajiv's story is a testament to a changing narrative around midlife, one that challenges the traditional notion of a 'midlife crisis' to instead suggest a 'midlife awakening.' Let's look at how media has shifted its portrayal of this period of life.

Changing Perspectives

How we perceive aging and midlife has drastically changed over the years. Archie Bunker's lament in the 1970s — 'They just wanna get rid of us old guys over 50 that's all, and put us out to pasture. Well I ain't ready to be pasteurized!' — encapsulates that era's perception of aging.

In the 1970s sitcom 'All in the Family', Archie and Edith Bunker, aged 46 and 48 at the series' start, depicted an older couple rooted in traditional values amid a rapidly evolving world. Fast forward to the mid-1980s, 'The Golden Girls' revolutionized television by featuring Bea Arthur, Betty White, Rue McClanahan, and Estelle Getty, all over the age of 50, leading vibrant, active lives. Then, 'Grace and Frankie' in 2015, pushing the narrative further. This series showcases its titular characters, played by Jane Fonda and Lily Tomlin in their mid-70s, not only as active participants in life but also as individuals reinventing themselves, breaking barriers in the tech industry, and exploring new relationships.

We have come a long way from the era when being over 50, 60, or even 70 was considered being 'pasture-ready.' 'Grace and Frankie' affirm that sometimes the best is yet to come, especially when you're not ready to be 'pasteurized'.

The Evolution of Leadership at Midlife

In my experience, and as seen in leaders like Rajiv, midlife brings about 'Three Winds of Change' — Physiological, Neurological, and Parental — that reshape not only our personal lives but also how we lead.

Physiological changes in midlife can significantly affect a leader's ability to stay present and effective. Diminished energy reserves make it challenging to maintain long hours or intense workloads. This was apparent in Rajiv's case, where he struggled with reduced stamina and increased fatigue. Executives might shift towards a more strategic and reflective leadership style, focusing on key decisions rather than on intensive day-to-day operations.

As health issues become more prevalent in midlife, executives might become more conscious of work-life balance, leading to a leadership style that emphasizes overall well-being. With a heightened awareness of their own health needs, executives might champion health and wellness initiatives within their organizations, leading to a more holistic approach to leadership.

Both men and women, in midlife, experience changes in hormones like estrogen and testosterone. These hormonal changes, while challenging, offer a gateway to reevaluate and recalibrate one's leadership approach. Leaders might be drawn to more frequent physical activity, dietary changes, and mindfulness practices.

Interestingly, a study by the Hartford Center for Mature Market Excellence and the MIT AgeLab supports this observation, noting that resilience tends to grow as we age. For instance, average Resilience in Midlife (RIM) scores rise from 64 in our 40s to 69 by our 60s, suggesting that the challenges of midlife could actually enhance our capacity to adapt and thrive.

There is another, intriguing aspect of the Physiological Wind of Change. Midlife is colored by a growing realization of potentially increased longevity. Reaching 50 might not signify an imminent retirement, but rather a significant mid-stage in one's career and lifespan. The prospect of living a healthy, productive life well beyond traditional retirement age can prompt a reevaluation of career arcs, such as my own choice to transition to executive coaching at 50. This drive for extended careers leads to increased investment in lifelong learning, skill development, and adaptability to new and evolving industries.

For those interested in a deeper dive into midlife's physical changes, Peter Attia's 'Outlive' offers insightful perspectives on longevity. His reflections resonate with my observations about the necessity of enjoying life while striving for perfection in our careers. Dr. Attia found himself obsessed with perfecting every aspect of his life, except truly enjoying it. I realized I saw much of his experiences reflected in my own.

A New Era of Wisdom

Midlife often brings a shift in how we process information. This is the Neurological Wind of Change. Experiences like slowed cognitive processing or challenges in quick memory recall. It might be harder to remember details, such as the specifics of a spreadsheet or the names of new colleagues. Many of my clients take more detailed notes during meetings. Some have found themselves strategically delegating memory-intensive tasks to their teams.

A significant development during this time is the enhanced connectivity between the left and right brain hemispheres, facilitating a more integrated and seamless blend of logical reasoning and creative thought. Recent neuroscience research, including a 2018 study by Fady Girgis et al., indicates that midlife's ongoing cognitive growth enhances our ability to process complex and opposing ideas. This suggests an increased capacity for understanding diverse perspectives, aiding in better decision-making and problem-solving in complex environments (Girgis et al., 2018). Our comfort with paradox increases, and our need for binary, black and white answers diminishes.

Think of the opposing thoughts Rajiv expressed: "I need to be fully committed to safety" versus "Full commitment to safety is impossible, because I can't be on everyone's back." His breakthrough came from holding the paradox, living with it as his mind searched for a solution. In Rajiv's case, the solution he settled on was revealed through another development in the midlife brain, emotional empathy.

The shift from cognitive to emotional empathy marks a critical development in midlife leadership. Research suggests that while older adults may see a decrease in cognitive empathy — the ability to understand the thoughts and feelings of others — they often maintain or even enhance their emotional empathy, resonating more deeply with the emotions of others. This transition is vividly illustrated in Rajiv's evolution as a leader. Initially focused on the cognitive aspects of enforcing safety protocols, Rajiv found himself perplexed by repeated accidents, wondering, "I don't understand what they could possibly be thinking. These accidents wouldn't happen if people just paid attention." However, as he tapped into his growing ability to connect with others emotionally, his perspective shifted. He began to see each accident as a personal story, acknowledging, "Each accident is a story of someone's life changing forever. It's my responsibility to feel that weight and act on it."

This nuanced understanding underscores the value of balancing cognitive strategies with emotional connectivity. Embracing emotional empathy not only strengthened relationships within Rajiv's organization but also bolstered morale, illustrating the profound impact of empathetic leadership on fostering a safety-first culture.

Understanding and adapting to this shift in empathy can significantly enrich a leader's approach, making them more adept at navigating the complex emotional dynamics of their teams and enhancing overall leadership effectiveness.

This cognitive shift also marks a time when leaders begin to blend their analytical skills with an enhanced or rediscovered talent for creativity. Leaders like Rajiv discover an increasing desire to combine their problem-solving abilities with a deeper capacity for creative expression. This combination takes shape in various forms, from crafting innovative solutions to engaging in artistic activities that merge intellect and emotion. These pursuits are more than just hobbies; they reflect a leader's growing emotional intelligence and intuitive insight.

You might notice these changes yourself — perhaps you're asking more questions or seeing connections you missed before. Embracing these shifts can open up new ways to lead and solve problems. Exploring an idea without the pressure of solving it immediately or reaching a conclusion might begin to feel exciting. You may also notice a change in your internal dialogue. Where you once might have thought, "This is the way it's always been done," you might now catch yourself thinking, "What if there's a better way to do this?"

While these beneficial neurological changes happen naturally at midlife, they can be undermined or suppressed. Adapting to these changes, rather than resisting them, is key to harnessing their full potential. For example, relying on a tried-and-tested work style can be advantageous in terms of efficiency and confidence, but can lead to cognitive stagnation, as the brain craves novelty and challenge. A more effective approach is to remain open to new experiences and learning opportunities. Stress, poor sleep, limited physical activity, an unhealthy diet, or excessive alcohol consumption can all significantly impair neuroplasticity. Acknowledging and addressing these lifestyle factors is essential for maintaining cognitive health and leadership effectiveness.

Rajiv's breakthrough came when he stopped resisting. His newfound emotional response and empathy towards his employees are typical of the impact of adapting to the Neurological Wind of Change. His journey from a stern, compliance-focused CEO to one who empathizes and connects with his employees on a personal level is a testament to the brain's evolving capacity for emotional intelligence and deeper connection-making.

"It was like walking through a fog that suddenly lifted," he said, "allowing me to see the distance between me and my team. That moment of clarity was pivotal; I realized that to truly lead, I needed to close that gap, to move beyond protocols and connect on a more human level."

Elkhonon Goldberg's 'The Wisdom Paradox' explores this

evolution in depth, offering insights that many find reflective of their own experiences in leadership roles at midlife. Goldberg is a renowned neuropsychologist whose work has significantly advanced our understanding of cognitive aging and neuroplasticity.

"Though the brain may age and change," Goldberg writes, "each phase of this progression presents new and different pleasures and advantages, as well as losses and trade-offs, in a natural progression, like the seasons."

Twenty years ago, in my early 40s, my morning drives to work were overshadowed by a persistent, unsettling dread. Despite our company's global success and a roster of top-tier bank clients (and lots to celebrate), I faced looming challenges that demanded unprecedented collaboration among our regional CEOs and functional heads, all experienced senior executives, some more challenging to manage than others. Despite my best efforts, I struggled to unite them—a failure that haunted me long after I sold the company. Reflecting on this, I realized that perhaps, at the time, I was simply too young to see the full picture.

Research from Grossmann et al. (2010) underscores a critical insight that resonates with my own experience—navigating complex social dynamics deepens significantly with age. The study shows that older individuals are more effective in using higher-order reasoning skills. These skills, crucial for leadership roles that demand strategic foresight and cross-functional cooperation, include perspective-taking, compromise, and recognizing knowledge limits.

It's now clear the wisdom required to foster a cohesive, enterprise-wide mindset among my team was just beyond my reach at the time. If you had asked me, "What do they want? What are their future ambitions, dreams and fears?" I wouldn't have had a clue.

Today, I often encounter leaders struggling to handle challenging individuals. One of the first questions I now ask is, "What does this person want?" Once prompted, my clients in their 50s quickly grasp the importance of recognizing the ambitions and vulnerabilities of others. It's as if a switch is flipped, and they can instantaneously shift from their earlier approach to a more empathetic and effective strategy.

As you navigate leadership challenges, especially when dealing with difficult individuals, it's crucial to dig deeper into their true motivations, with empathy. Embracing these emerging skills could be the key to a successful second half of life.

This understanding of the brain's evolution — much like the unfolding seasons — naturally leads us to the next phase of our journey: the seasons of parenting. Let's delve into the Parental Wind of Change, unveiling how our leadership stage mirrors our parenting stage.

The Parental Influence on Leadership

This third wind of change is actually the first that became clear to me early in my coaching practice. I began noticing how an executive's current leadership style often reflected their parenting stage.

A first-time CEO complained about his team's lack of initiative, likening it to dealing with teenagers. He reflected and realized that he was projecting his parenting approach onto his employees, expecting independence but inadvertently fostering dependency.

Another manager often withheld information from her team, believing she was protecting them from unnecessary details. Yet, she found their persistent questions frustrating, reminding her of dealing with her own curious kids. The question "Why?" especially annoyed her. Laughing, she acknowledged the parallel.

Another leader, the father of three teenagers, navigated remote work by adopting tight supervision, similar to the close watch he kept on his young children. 'Processes are crucial,' he insisted, fearing that without them, people might slack off. This scenario echoes a broader pattern in many workplaces, suggesting that well-meaning rules can sometimes result in employees feeling micromanaged.

Leadership often feels like parenting because both roles share a fundamental emotional connection centered on care, responsibility, and the desire to see others succeed and grow. Searching 'leadership and parenting' online yields over half a billion hits, far exceeding topics like C-suite leadership and career transitions.

How does this relate to midlife? And, for that matter, how does it relate to midlife leadership?

Senior executives in their 40s and 50s are in a phase of life that often coincides with parenting teenagers on the verge of leaving home. Parenting in this 'in-between' stage involves a complex mix of independence and dependency. The challenge of letting go, acknowledging a child's growing independence, and trusting their ability to adapt and thrive in diverse situations underscores this evolution. It compels parents to redefine their roles and relationships, fostering a new dynamic that celebrates the emerging adult in their child while still providing guidance and support from the sidelines. In other words, it's a lot like leadership.

This is a big shift from parenting younger children, focused more on direct supervision, instruction, and decision-making. It mirrors the management versus leadership debate.

Senior executive leaders are also navigating a similar 'in-between' stage at work, still balancing Key Performance Indicators (KPIs), clear directives, and an "if you do this, then you get that" management mindset. At the same time, they're evolving into a mature leadership style, mirroring parents whose children have become independent adults, learning that inspiration and empowerment are their most effective tools. Nothing else is nearly as effective. Leadership, unlike management, is less about "if you do this, then you get that" and more about "here's why this matters."

With the Parental Wind of Change come poignantly introspective questions: "How do I let go, trusting they have the tools to succeed? If they don't want my advice, how am I still relevant? What value do I now have?" These questions resonate throughout this book's anecdotes and stories. See how Rajiv grapples with commitment? Initially, he felt he had to monitor every employee closely — a surprisingly common scenario in process-heavy organizations.

There are countless examples, from the need for overly detailed progress updates and strict internet guidelines to managerial sign-offs for small expenses or mandatory doctor's notes for short sick leaves. And let's not forget team-building events that more often than not, feel like a requirement rather than a choice.

In this same vein, rolling out values and mission statements often mirrors the setting of household rules, adopting a top-down approach that whispers, "We know best, and these are the values we want you to live by," further underlining a culture of directive governance over collaborative engagement.

Management and leadership books, literature, processes, and training programs are frequently authored by individuals in the earlier stages of their parenting journey. This context subtly and inadvertently influences their content, mirroring their current parenting stage.

Walking through an organization overly cluttered with performance metrics, rules, and tight controls, always causes me to suspect that the top levels of managers still have kids at home.

This over-management, while rooted in a desire to guide, can often result in diminished accountability and ownership, an indication that an organization might have crossed into the realm of infantilization. A large-scale internet study shows that treating competent adults as if they were children leads (no surprise here) to diminished agency, responsibility, and ownership — feelings that can cripple a team's morale and effectiveness ('Infantilization across the life span,' by Epstein, Roberts, and Johnson of the American Institute for Behavioral Research and Technology, 2022). Other negative outcomes the researchers found include increased depression and anxiety, anger directed toward authority figures, lower self-esteem, and damaged relationships.

Fortunately, as we adapt to our children's growing independence, we begin to view our teams not just as subordinates but as capable, mature individuals. We learn to step back, resist the urge to micromanage, and empower others with the authority to take initiative. As we witness our children forming their own identities and values as adults, it can prompt us to reflect on our own legacy and the values we want to instill in our families and our organizations. These shifts pave the way for a more dynamic, empathetic, and effective leadership style.

Almost every leader I've worked with has seen a dramatic change once they realize they've been applying their parenting mindset at work without even knowing it. Our current leadership style often reflects our parenting stage; awareness instantly dissolves this mirror.

A Time for Reflection and Growth

In summarizing the transformative journey of midlife leadership through *The Three Winds of Change*, we can distill the essence of each wind into a single word. The *Physiological Wind of Change* brings 'Resilience,' as leaders adapt to their changing bodies and health. The *Neurological Wind of Change* is encapsulated by 'Wisdom,' reflecting the deepened understanding, emotional intelligence, and cognitive flexibility that leaders gain. Lastly, the *Parental Wind of Change* can be summarized as 'Empathy,' mirroring the shift in parenting roles to a more empowering leadership style. These words — Resilience, Wisdom, and Empathy — capture the core benefits of the midlife transformation for senior leaders.

As I reflect on the *Three Winds of Change*, I recall a defining moment in my own journey. A ropes course, seemingly a simple team-building activity, turned out to be a crucible for my own leadership transformation. I was forty-eight, very close to Rajiv's age. The course was designed to challenge and build trust, but it ended up revealing more about myself and my style of leadership than I had anticipated. This experience became a pivotal exploration of my leadership approach, unveiling a significant blind spot — a story I'm eager to share in the following pages.

Crucible Moments in Mastery

The final exercise of the ropes course required crossing a precarious bridge blindfolded, with only the guidance of a partner. My partner was a young woman with a profound fear of heights. She struggled and dropped out of some of the earlier activities, and now she was tasked with guiding me, the blindfolded one, across the bridge.

She was petrified. I encouraged her, even begged her to move, but she wouldn't budge.

At that moment, I experienced an intense need to override her hesitation with my action. Perhaps it was an innate drive to fix situations, a lack of trust in her abilities, or perhaps a deeper, unconscious desire to assert control in weighty situations. My instincts kicked in and I took charge. I got in front of her and told her to hold my harness. I then led us across the bridge whilst I was still blindfolded. At that moment, it felt like a triumph, but the facilitator was furious. She poked her finger at my chest when I got back down. "What the hell were you doing up there?"

"I got the job done," I said.

What the facilitator said next has always stayed with me. "You sucked the courage out of her. And you used it as fuel to drive your need to be a hero... You wasted... WASTED... the opportunity to trust someone else... and learn what it feels like to let go of control." She began walking away in disgust, then turned around and said, "Leadership is the unwavering conviction, deep in your bones, that every person possesses immense courage. But what you did up there was act like a 'Courage Vampire,' draining her courage to bolster your own need to be seen as a hero. Instead of feeding off her fear, you could have fueled her courage."

My reaction was the same as Rajiv's when we first explored his level of commitment — I got angry. But over the next day, I stewed in everything the facilitator said. I realised the facilitator was right. Being a 'Courage Vampire' wasn't something I had done consciously, but by taking charge, I had indeed sucked away my partner's opportunity to overcome her fear. This moment was a stark reminder that leadership isn't just about leading the way but also about lighting the path for others to find their own courage.

My actions had indeed deprived my partner of a crucial growth opportunity. It struck me that my incessant need to take charge and my belief that my worth hinged on being indispensable fostered an unintentional dynamic of co-dependency. I needed to be needed. The introspection led me to confront a 'Secret Saboteur' that had been weighing me down: the belief that my value as a leader and as a person was in taking charge and solving problems. This belief had subtly undermined my ability to truly empower others and trust in their capabilities.

From there, the deeper epiphany was a step away, the realization that our greatest value is in having the unwavering conviction in the capabilities of others; learning to let go, to trust, and to fully empower others. The more you give away, the more you embrace.

This paradox encapsulates the counterintuitive truth that by relinquishing control, by trusting in others to take the lead in their own growth and learning, and by prioritizing their development over one's own immediate influence or outcomes — whether as a leader, parent, coach, or mentor — we gain something far more valuable.

This approach not only fosters growth in others — by allowing room for others to explore, fail, learn, and ultimately, grow — but also enriches our own personal and professional development, as we gradually discover that our real value as a human being lies not in the ability to solve problems or direct outcomes but in the capacity to instill confidence, foster autonomy, and facilitate growth in others.

The ropes course became a vivid metaphor for the 'Three Winds of Change' sweeping through my midlife — physiological transformations, neurological reconfigurations, and a shifting parental landscape. These winds were the very catalysts for the profound epiphany I experienced.

My body was changing, and I didn't want to admit it. Stress was pressing down on me more than before. My world felt heavy. Nights had become increasingly restless. I would often wake up at 2:30 am, drenched in sweat, and my mind laden with work-related worries. Despite efforts to manage my diet, cholesterol levels stubbornly crept up. Regular client dinners made sticking to healthier choices a challenge. Resisting the physiological changes, pretending they could be overcome, I was more than eager to push my way through the ropes course, even blindfolded, to prove to myself that I still had the physical stamina of my younger self.

On the neurological front, my approach to problem-solving was evolving. I often asked my team emotionally charged questions: "What keeps our clients awake at night?" and "So what, who cares, why us?" These weren't just strategic queries; they aimed to tap into a deeper, emotional understanding of our clients' needs. Years later I discovered that this shift towards integrating analytical thinking with emotional intelligence is a hallmark of midlife, reflecting a tighter interplay between the brain's left and right hemispheres.

Then there was my personal life, which was very much in flux. My daughters were adults and my sixteen-year-old son was rapidly growing up. Frequent work travel had made me miss much of their upbringing. After divorce, living separately from my son added to the heaviness of loss. At work, I'd catch myself calling colleagues by my children's names, revealing how my parental instincts were blending into my professional life. This mix-up was more than a simple error; it signified how my brain was processing these significant personal changes.

I remember very clearly in a follow-up coaching session with the facilitator, as I unpacked the insights that were developing within me, where I shared how heavy and burdensome everything felt, at work, at home, and seemingly everywhere. She listened quietly, then simply asked what sports I practiced. "I lift weights," I smiled sheepishly as the penny dropped.

The ropes course was a pivotal moment, illuminating the changes that were reshaping my life and leadership, propelling me towards embracing a more empowering leadership philosophy and a deeper understanding of my own evolving identity.

Every 'Let me handle this' from a leader is a Courage Vampire's dinner bell. This realization crystallized for me the importance of truly nurturing courage and autonomy, not just in those we lead but within ourselves as well. It's a reminder that true leadership is about empowering others to cross their own bridges, even when we're tempted to lead the way. Leadership is not leading; it's believing in those who follow.

As leaders, recognizing and adapting to the winds of change can propel us towards a more fulfilling and impactful phase of our careers and lives. It's about harnessing the full potential of midlife and being aware of the Secret Saboteurs that can hinder our growth and development.

Secret Saboteurs — Subtle Barriers to Personal and Professional Growth at Midlife

This section reveals hidden beliefs that senior executives often hold, which may seem conducive to success but can actually hinder personal and professional growth. These beliefs come from past achievements and traditional ideas of leadership, but they can prevent flexibility, stifle emotional depth, and undermine a focus on people, which are crucial to grow and lead effectively.

"Being a strong leader means having a clear and unwavering vision." While clarity of vision is commendable, it might inadvertently narrow one's perspective, and in the process inhibit the hemispheric connections that develop at midlife. What if embracing uncertainty became your most powerful tool for leadership, allowing space for creativity and innovation to flourish?

"I must have the answers; otherwise, what value do I offer?" This perspective might overlook the richness that collaborative wisdom and shared problem-solving bring to the table. Can you imagine the breakthroughs that could occur if your primary role shifted from being the one who answers to the one who asks the most insightful questions?

"I prefer to oversee critical tasks myself to ensure quality." This preference, while well-intentioned, might inadvertently limit your team's growth opportunities and your ability to delegate effectively. Could the act of stepping back not only amplify your team's potential but also redefine your leadership as one that builds leaders rather than followers?

"My productivity and success reflect my dedication to my role." Linking productivity directly with personal value might narrow one's definition of success and overlook the multifaceted aspects of leadership growth. What if your legacy was measured not by the volume of work you produced but by the depth of impact you made on others' lives and careers?

"The clock is ticking to achieve all my career goals." This time-bound perspective might rush decisions and overlook the depth of experiences available in a prolonged career. How could adopting a lens of 'time abundance' rather than 'time scarcity' transform your approach to leadership and open up unforeseen paths to success?

Conclusion: Embracing Transformation in Midlife Leadership

Rajiv's journey not only underscores the significant shift in leadership perspective that often occurs in midlife but also demonstrates

how this transformation can complement and enhance traditional leadership metrics. Rather than moving away from an exclusive
emphasis on traditional metrics such as financial performance, productivity, and safety records, the midlife transformation integrates
these with a heightened focus on introspection, empathy, and the
development of deeper, more meaningful connections within the
workplace. This holistic approach does not diminish the value of
traditional metrics but enriches them, creating a more balanced and
effective leadership style that values both tangible outcomes and the
intangible qualities that foster a thriving workplace culture.

In chapter two, we will explore six leadership superpowers that
emerge from the perfect storm of midlife's winds of change.

Chapter Two
Unfolding the DNA of Leadership Mastery

"WHEN we laugh and play
with our many identities,
when we see that all of these
are masks,
when we let go
of outdated labels
even if we still love them
very much,
then,
our genuine, authentic self
can shine through,
more complex,
more beautiful,
than any label
could possibly capture."

— **Nicole Parker**

Narratives of Leadership Evolution

It was a cloudy afternoon when Nicole Parker and I found ourselves seated down for coffee in a quiet corner of a cafe. Her brows were furrowed in deep thought, her fingers tapping anxiously on the table.

She huffed, shaking her head, "I don't get it. We're outperforming everyone else – yet here I am, still labeled as 'interim.' What more are they looking for?" Her voice trailed off, a mix of frustration and confusion coloring her tone.

Taking a sip of my coffee, I bought myself a moment to ponder. "That does sound frustrating. It sounds like they might be expecting more from you."

Nicole paused, her eyes scanning the cafe as if seeking answers in its corners. She leaned forward, her voice dropping to a more intimate tone, "Exactly. They won't say what they're looking for. It's like I'm banging my head against a wall here."

She tapped her fingers against her cup, a gesture of contained energy and frustration. "They've tagged me as 'intense' or 'prickly' — it's as if the assertiveness that brought me this far is a problem." Nicole lowered her voice. "On one hand, I know I've been successful because of my decisiveness. But on the other hand, I'm wondering if that's enough anymore. Do I need to drive even harder? But would I then be more 'prickly'?" She used air quotes. "God, I hate that word!"

She paused, her hand moving through the air as though searching for the right words. "And honestly..." her voice trailed off, vulnerability flashing across her face, "I've had some health issues and now I wonder if it's all starting to take a toll. Reading your draft, the idea of 'Physiological' changes struck a chord."

Nicole had insights into the 'three winds' from an early manuscript draft — Physiological, Neurological, and Parental. How would she interpret these influences in her own life?

Navigating the Body's New Rhythms

Nicole's gaze drifted off as if she were peering into a distance that only she could see. "It's a struggle, all these changes hitting me suddenly. All at once," she paused, her voice catching slightly as if the words themselves were hurdles. "It's like midlife suddenly rang a gong — out of nowhere, and my body just started changing." She clasped her hands together tightly, as if trying not to lose control of her inner turmoil.

Sensing the tension in her voice, I leaned in slightly. "Could you elaborate on that a bit?" I asked gently.

"Long story short..." She hesitated for a minute, collecting her thoughts. As I paid attention to her body language, I waited quietly, offering my full attention, and signifying to her that I'm following her thoughts, and she can take her time. She found the willpower, and continued, "My doctor says I have hormonal imbalances. It's affecting everything — my mood, my decisions, even how I interact with others," she said, her voice steady. I nodded, encouraging her to continue. "I wonder, is this a temporary setback or a lasting change? Am I losing my competitive edge?" There was a hint of frustration in her voice. "I've always been at the front, leading. Now, I find myself second-guessing."

Her eyes met mine, as if searching for answers.

Leaning forward, I gently probed. "If you had a question right now, that would encapsulate everything you're concerned about... what would that be?"

Nicole's gaze was sharp and focused. "I feel like I'm losing my grip, you know? It's like I'm playing with a handicap—not at full strength at all." She sighed heavily, a sign of her inner struggle. Nicole was amid a crucible moment – an intense personal challenge where her leadership identity was being tested and reshaped.

I reflected, "Redefining yourself is tough, especially with your experience."

She nodded firmly. "I can't afford to be seen as weak, not in my position."

I asked, "Are these challenges pushing you to double down on your approach, making you seem more intense?"

She gripped her hands tightly. "My team isn't keeping pace. I'm concerned. If I lose my edge, what then? It feels like I'm being cornered into changing who I am."

"I understand," I said. "Perhaps it's about finding a way to balance your strengths — even the way your strengths are evolving — with the need to collaborate effectively and continue delivering results."

Nicole straightened up, her face set in determination. "I won't let that slide. That's non-negotiable," she said, her tone firm but her eyes betraying a flicker of doubt.

There it was — the 'Secret Saboteur' at play, a concept we'd explored earlier. This deeply ingrained belief that her aggressive competitive approach was the only path to success was now holding her back.

The crux of Nicole's dilemma is one which is shared by many leaders at midlife, and it lies in incorporating their tried-and-true attributes with evolving skills vital for ongoing success. For leaders like Nicole, the challenge lies in harmonizing a formidable, results-oriented approach with the finesse for teamwork and adaptability. It's about not losing the tenacity and drive that fueled her rise, while cultivating the humility to engage with and adapt to new dynamics and perspectives.

With a little prodding, Nicole shared more about her frustration. "You know, it's always been about being the best, pushing the hardest. That's me – that's how I got here. Can you really get to the top and stay there without being a bit of a bulldozer? I've always been that person who stands out because of my drive, and now I'm being asked to step back and blend in a bit more. That's not me."

"Maybe what the board is looking for," I offered, "is your ability to channel that intensity into the broader success of the company, not just your unit. Your iron will is undeniable..."

She laughed, "and I'm lacking the humility." Then she paused and looked very thoughtful again. "I see what you mean. But the feedback was vague. Prickly, they say? I mean, how do I even begin to address that without losing my edge?"

"Consider," I gently suggested, "that they might be seeking signs of a more inclusive leadership style."

She laughed again, but there was a bittersweet quality to it.

"Actually, wait," she said. "I know this feeling. It's like I'm back in college."

The Mind's New Horizons

Nicole gazed out the window. "Back in high school, being a soccer star was about scoring goals myself, being the hero. It was a great feeling, you know? I was so competitive and focused on winning at all costs, even if it meant stepping on my teammates' toes to get there. But that was okay, because I was the best, and that's all that mattered to me."

She paused with a slight, thoughtful smile, her posture relaxed and poised, and her fingers tapping lightly on the side of her coffee mug.

"In college, the game changed," she continued. "I thought I was going to be the star again. But the expectations were different. They wanted me to be a team player, working together to win. I felt like I was losing my edge, my ability to shine as an individual. It was frustrating. I couldn't adjust and eventually quit soccer. Reflecting on that now, I see parallels with my current challenges in embracing collaboration over individual triumph."

Now, years later, with this recent feedback about her collaboration skills, Nicole was getting a second chance to address the personal transformation she didn't go through as a young adult — a second chance to become a team player.

"That's really interesting," I observed, leaning in a bit. "You're drawing lines between your competitive soccer days and your leadership style now — that's what I'd call a midlife revelation. It's like gaining the wisdom to see the bigger picture, isn't it?

Nicole laughed. "Ah, the Neurological Wind of Change at work!"

I said, "It's fascinating, right? Feeling your thought patterns shift, making these new connections?"

She nodded. "I feel that. It's like... my mind is weaving things together in new ways."

"Exactly!" I exclaimed. "Just moments ago, as you talked about soccer, your mind was connecting different parts of your life, past and present. You're looking back, re-evaluating experiences, seeing patterns, and linking them to where you are today. This deep reflection can bring a lot of insights."

Nicole nodded thoughtfully. "Instead of fighting these changes, what if I embraced them? What if I saw this as an opportunity to evolve, not just as a leader but in how I view the world?"

"What would happen if you did?"

Her eyes darted back and forth, a manifestation of cognitive processes where the brain is searching for information, recalling memories, or constructing a response. Nicole's expression softened down eventually. "You know," she began slowly, "this whole conversation... it's like a lightbulb moment. I've been so caught up in resisting change, trying to hold on to who I was, rather than exploring what this new phase could bring."

I nodded, encouraging her to continue her train of thought. "Sounds like the start of something deeply inspiring."

Her gaze shifted out the window, reflecting emerging possibilities. "Embracing this journey..." she repeated quietly, as if etching the words into her mind. "It's time to lean in." A new voice could be heard from her, like a relentless openness to the unknown.

"Did you notice the shift?" I asked, smiling.

She laughed. "Yes, I did."

I exclaimed, "There's a new tone in your voice — something that balances humility with determination. It's compelling."

Nicole nodded, a wide grin on her face, and she jabbed her index finger at me. "That's exactly right!"

We had talked about two of the midlife Winds of Change — Physiological and Neurological — leaving me curious about how Nicole experienced the Parental Wind of Change without being a mother.

Parenthood's Echo in Leadership

I leaned forward, elbows on the table. "Nicole, you mentioned earlier that you felt the impact of all three Winds of Change."

She smiled. "And you're wondering about the third."

I nodded.

Nicole took a deep breath, her posture momentarily tightening as if bracing herself. "With everything that's happened, the divorce, and my relationship with my step-children, it's brought up a lot of thoughts about family," she said, her voice a shade softer. "Especially about how these personal aspects influence my approach to leadership."

Her gaze drifted slightly to the side, not quite meeting mine, as she seemed to be accessing deeper, more introspective thoughts. "I've always said I had no regrets about prioritizing my career," she said, her voice carrying a trace of uncertainty, "but sometimes, I do wonder." There was something else in her voice, which I couldn't quite put my finger on.

"Lately, I've been considering the paths I didn't take." She paused, and there it was again — a wistful expression flitting across her face so briefly you might have imagined it, suggesting something else, not just regret.

"My step-kids were almost grown when I entered their lives. Sometimes, I wonder about the impact I might have had if things were different, if I had gotten closer to them." As she finished, Nicole offered a small, somewhat strained smile, an attempt to reassure both of us that she was at peace with her choices, even as her fingers lightly traced the edge of her sleeve, a subtle outlet for the emotions stirring just beneath the surface. Guilt. Just a small hint of guilt. That's what I was sensing.

"And now, with your leadership role," I interjected, "do you find these reflections influencing your decisions?"

Nicole began sounding contemplative. "It's broader than just family — it's about nurturing relationships, whether at home or work. The skills overlap more than I realized."

"That's a significant realization," I noted. "How is this influencing your view of leadership?"

She looked at me. "What's challenging is this feeling of paths closing. It's a new awareness for me. I didn't feel this when I was younger. Now, it's making me ponder the paths I'm setting for my future."

Nicole leaned back as resolve was beginning to reemerge. "I'm reflecting on the opportunities I might be missing now, considering how today's choices shape tomorrow."

I was absorbing her reflections. "These are profound insights. Do you feel they're changing you as a leader?"

Nicole paused, considering her response. "In theory, they should make me a better leader. More considerate of long-term impacts and more patient."

"But?" I prompted.

She sighed slightly. "But honestly, I worry that in becoming more introspective, I might be losing some of my decisiveness — my edge."

"Balancing assertiveness with empathy," I said, "it's a tough act. You're trying to find that middle ground without compromising who you are."

Nicole nodded. "Exactly. I'm grappling with this fear that embracing introspection and empathy means losing my edge." She laughed, a hint of irony in her voice. "I guess it's about finding a balance between different aspects of myself."

I smiled, recognizing her journey. "Embracing the complexities of who we are," I said. "Especially as we grow and evolve."

She took a deep breath, a look of understanding dawning. "Embracing the ambiguity and paradox," she mused, "that's the real challenge, isn't it? Finding peace in the complexities of midlife."

I nodded. "I couldn't agree more. I think it's part of the beauty of midlife – the ability to hold and value these paradoxes."

She was now smiling fully with her eyes, radiating a genuine sense of determination. "I can do that."

The Physiological Wind of Change

As Nicole navigated midlife, she faced not just the typical signs of aging but significant hormonal imbalances that began to influence her mood and decision-making. Previously sharp and decisive, she now found herself wrestling with an inconsistent energy level and fluctuating moods, challenging her sense of control and forcing her to rethink her leadership approach.

In response to these changes, Nicole shifted from relying solely on her high energy and assertiveness to embracing a more nuanced leadership style. She began to strategically delegate more responsibilities, ensuring she maintained her effectiveness while managing her energy to prevent burnout.

This phase of Nicole's life is revealing the subtle yet profound shifts that come with aging. As her physical stamina evolves, so does her emotional and psychological resilience, uncovering hidden strengths that were once overshadowed by her youthful vigor.

As Nicole discovers new forms of grace and acceptance in this phase of her life, it invites us to reflect on our own experiences. What unexpected forms of grace are you discovering as you age? What hidden strengths are emerging as you adapt to your body's new rhythms?

The Neurological Wind of Change

Nicole noticed subtle shifts in her cognitive abilities. While she occasionally experienced moments of forgetfulness and a slightly slower processing speed, these changes prompted her to become more contemplative. Her thinking evolved, integrating her once rapid-fire decision-making skills with a more deliberate and reflective approach. This newfound depth of thought enabled her to approach problems more holistically, combining her accumulated wisdom with fresh, innovative strategies.

The evolution in her thought process not only deepened her emotional intelligence but also transformed her interactions with her team. Nicole found herself engaging in more meaningful dialogues, considering her team's perspectives more fully, and fostering a collaborative environment that valued empathy alongside hard data.

Reflecting on Nicole's journey and her integration of past soccer experiences with her current insights, consider your own path: How do the blending of your past experiences and present insights shape your view of the future? What new understandings emerge from revisiting familiar thoughts under the light of recent changes in your life?

In moments of quiet reflection, Nicole discovered new curiosities awakening within her, leading to insights that melded logic with intuition in ways she hadn't previously understood. How do such changes manifest in your own life, blending thought and feeling into a new tapestry of understanding?

The Parental Wind of Change

In contrast to Rajiv's experience in Chapter One, Nicole's relationship with parenthood presents a different, yet equally insightful, narrative. As someone who navigated midlife without having biological children but experienced the role of a stepparent, Nicole faced unique challenges and insights. Her journey, unlike Rajiv's direct correlation of parental transformation with professional leadership evolution, involved reflecting on the absence of a traditional parenting role and its implications on her leadership style.

Initially, Nicole approached her role as a stepparent with the same assertiveness and command she valued in the boardroom. However, she soon realized that her teenage stepchildren responded better to empathy and understanding than to authority and control. The challenging process of adapting her style uncovered her capacity for nurturing, which had been less demanded in her professional life.

Unlike Rajiv, who found a direct correlation between parenting and professional leadership, Nicole's journey involved a subtler, yet profound, evolution. She learned that leadership, much like non-biological parenting, often requires a pivot from exerting control to facilitating growth and understanding.

Both Rajiv and Nicole, despite their different journeys, encounter common themes in their midlife transformations, highlighting the need for adaptability, empathy, and a deeper understanding of their impact on others.

Reflecting on her step-parenting, Nicole recognized missed opportunities to connect more deeply with her stepchildren. This acknowledgment spurred a broader realization about her leadership style: true influence often stems from nurturing potential rather than directing it.

As you contemplate your own roles—be they parental, mentorship, or leadership — consider how nurturing has reshaped your approach. How has the shift from controlling to empowering others revealed new dimensions of your character? What lessons from personal relationships have you applied to your leadership to foster growth and empathy?

Adapt or Resist the Winds of Change

Those who embrace these Winds unlock Six Midlife Leadership Superpowers, each contributing uniquely to personal and professional growth. These include Humility and Iron Will, which balance strength with grace; Continual Rebirth, encouraging ongoing self-renewal; Boundless Ideation, fostering creativity; Total Ownership, emphasizing accountability; Timeless Impact, focusing on enduring influence; and Life Synergy, which harmonizes personal and professional life.

Leaders who resist these Winds often find themselves struggling to stay relevant. They risk becoming entrenched in outdated methods, which can lead to reduced team morale, decreased innovation, and ultimately, a diminished capacity to connect with colleagues and clients in meaningful ways.

Reflecting on adaptation and growth, poet Mary Oliver captures the essence of embracing life's challenges in her poem 'Halleluiah.' She writes, 'And have you too been trudging like that, sometimes almost forgetting how wondrous the world is and how miraculously kind some people can be? And have you too decided that probably nothing important is ever easy? Not, say, for the first sixty years. Halleluiah, I'm sixty now, and even a little more, and some days I feel I have wings.'

Mary Oliver's words resonated deeply with me as I was undergoing midlife transformations, reminding me that while the journey is fraught with challenges, it is also filled with opportunities for rediscovery and growth. Like Oliver, leaders can find that with age comes not just challenges but also the 'wings' of freedom and insight

With these thoughts in mind, let's explore the six leadership traits nurtured by the Winds of Change. How can these superpowers guide us toward a leadership style characterized by resilience, empathy, and adaptability? Let's delve deeper.

Humility and Iron Will

Midlife often ushers in a perfect storm that softens us with humility while still driving us forward with iron will. This superpower marries the wisdom to accept personal limitations with the strength to tackle life's challenges head-on, much like Jim Collins' concept of Level 5 Leadership, which harmonizes personal humility with professional will.

This trait is a transition from the bold determination of early career stages, to a wise and mature leadership approach in midlife. It values asking difficult questions and navigating uncertainties, rather than always being expected to have the right answers. Leaders embodying this trait enrich their strong will with humility, resulting in resilience in uncertainty and embracing diverse perspectives.

Julio Olalla, the founder of ontological coaching, echoes this sentiment: "*Knowledge is a love affair with answers. Wisdom is a love affair with questions.*"

David Whyte, a poet and corporate philosopher, emphasizes asking "beautiful questions" in challenging situations. In one of his recollections, Whyte shared a transformative experience with his adolescent daughter. Initially, he approached a delicate conversation with a fixed mindset, prepared to assert his parental authority. However, as any parent of teens can imagine, he soon recognized this is ineffective. Consequently, Whyte carefully prepared a setting conducive to an open dialogue—a tray laden with tea and cookies, creating a warm and inviting atmosphere. In this more relaxed and respectful environment, he asked his daughter, not as a father commanding respect, but as a humble listener, to articulate what she needed from him during this phase of her life. This marked a significant departure from a one-way conversation, to one of mutual exchange. Not only did he need to exercise humility and recognize his limitations as a parent, but he also needed the iron will to face the truths of their changing relationship, and his daughter's growing independence.

Other notable leaders like Bill Gates, Steve Jobs, and Howard Schultz exemplify this trait. Gates' evolution from a competitive tech leader to a global philanthropist, Jobs' refined leadership upon returning to Apple, and Schultz's focus on social issues and employee welfare at Starbucks, demonstrate how successful leaders can integrate humility with determination to achieve a more profound impact.

These shifts in leadership traits are not just psychological but are underpinned by neurological changes during midlife. The maturation of the brain's prefrontal cortex, which enhances emotional regulation, and improvements in the anterior cingulate cortex and mirror neuron system, boost our capacity for empathy and understanding.

David Whyte vividly captures the power of questions, stating: "*The ability to ask beautiful questions, often in very unbeautiful moments, is one of the great disciplines of a human life. And a beautiful question starts to shape your identity as much by asking it as it does by having it answered.*"

Secret Saboteurs — Subtle barriers to developing this superpower:

- "As a leader, I must always appear decisive and unyielding to maintain respect and authority. Showing flexibility or doubt could be seen as a sign of weakness." This suggests a fear of losing credibility or authority by not adhering strictly to established patterns. How might embracing bold adaptability and openness to new perspectives not only enhance your leadership but transform the culture within your team? If nurturing curiosity and embracing uncertainty became your team's greatest strengths, what astonishing innovations and solutions might emerge?
- "If I question the methods or strategies that have worked in the past, it might undermine my past successes and decision-making abilities." This implies a fear of invalidating previous achievements by embracing change or admitting that past methods might no longer be the best approach. What specific fears arise when you consider embracing the power of questioning past strategies? Envision a future where reevaluating past successes is celebrated as a cornerstone of your team's culture. How does this profound shift enhance your approach to leadership and decision-making?
- "Changing my approach or admitting uncertainty could lead my team to question my leadership and capabilities." This reflects a concern that embracing ambiguity or change might be perceived as a lack of competence or direction. How would

you describe the dynamic equilibrium between confidence in decision-making and the courageous embrace of ambiguity? Where do you currently stand on this spectrum, and where do you aspire to be?

Practical exercises to enhance 'Humility and Iron Will':
- *Solicit diverse feedback.* Regularly ask for feedback from a wide range of people. Opt for one-on-one sessions to hone your skill of creating a safe environment where others feel comfortable sharing honest opinions. Foster a feedback culture by showing eagerness and curiosity to learn how others perceive your leadership style.
- *Engage actively in cross-cultural experiences.* Proactively seek opportunities to work with or lead teams from different cultural backgrounds. This could involve participating in international projects, attending cross-cultural training sessions, or even living in a different country for a period. Actively engage in these experiences to understand and appreciate different cultural norms and practices, uncover your own biases, and enhance your adaptability.
- *Set challenges outside your comfort zone.* Make it a habit to do something regularly that scares you. Explore unfamiliar situations and learn to navigate the discomfort that comes with them. Embrace the uncertainty and ambiguity of these experiences to build resilience and adaptability.

Continual Rebirth

Growing older teaches us the fine art of letting go, showing us the beauty of traveling light.

Continual Rebirth is the ongoing process of personal and professional transformation. It consists of actively embracing evolving roles, drawing from diverse life experiences, and using introspection to innovate and adapt, a characteristic unique to the reflective phase of midlife.

The journey of midlife often brings a profound shift in both personal and professional identities. This phase is marked by embracing roles that are evolving and possessing a readiness to let go of old identities. Leaders in midlife leverage introspection gained from years of experience, to navigate these changes. Herman Hesse, the German-Swiss poet and novelist, encapsulates this experience with his insight: *"Some of us think holding on makes us strong, but sometimes it is letting go."*

Harvard psychologist and professor Robert Kegan, the founder of adult development theory, writes, *"Every transition involves to some extent the killing off of the old self."* This letting go can culminate in Kegan's fifth and highest order of adult development, which he calls the self-transforming mind, characterized by the ability to hold multiple perspectives, embrace contradictions, and remain open to transformation.

In their careers, senior leaders undergo numerous transformations, evolving from roles like Entry-Level Employee, Team Leader, and Department Head, to Corporate Executive. Similarly, personal life changes, from New Parent to Empty-Nester, mirror this professional evolution. Having experienced such a range of identities, midlife leaders understand the impermanence of these labels, making the concept of Continual Rebirth more intuitive. They are uniquely positioned to seize opportunities for reinventing both themselves and their organizations. As we age, we become masters of letting go, because we've had so much practice letting go of so much stuff.

American poet Mary Oliver's "Journey" beautifully captures this transition. *"But little by little, as you left their voice behind, the stars began to burn through the sheets of clouds, and there was a new voice which you slowly recognized as your own, that kept you company as you strode deeper and deeper into the world, determined to do the only thing you could do — determined to save the only life that you could save."*

This Midlife Leadership Superpower aligns with the natural tendency for introspection and transformation. It encourages leaders to use their life experiences as a foundation for continual personal and professional development, enhancing their leadership and the growth of their organizations.

Secret Saboteurs — Subtle barriers to developing this superpower:

- "Constantly evolving and adopting new identities might make me appear inconsistent or unreliable in my leadership role." This reflects a fear that continual personal and professional transformation could be perceived as a lack of steadfastness or clear direction. Imagine a world where your constant evolution is seen as your greatest strength. What qualities or successes become highlighted in this new perspective? When have you witnessed someone else's transformation be a catalyst for positive change in a team or organization? What did you learn from their journey?

- "If I let go of past roles and identities that have defined my success, I may lose my sense of self and the respect I've earned." This suggests a concern that moving away from familiar labels and achievements might lead to a loss of identity and recognition. Reflect on a role or identity you've moved on from. What new opportunities or strengths emerged as a result? What aspects of your current identity are you most afraid of losing? Why? How might letting go open the door to something equally or more valuable?

- "Reinventing myself and my approach could lead to uncertainty and instability within the team or organization." This implies a fear that personal transformation might create confusion or lack of continuity for the team. Can you think of a scenario where reinventing yourself could actually stabilize or revitalize your team or organization? How do you balance the need for personal growth with the need for organizational stability? Can these be mutually supportive rather than mutually exclusive?

Practical exercises to embrace an attitude of 'Continual Rebirth':

- *Challenge fixed identity labels with the 'I am not this, I am not that' exercise.* Identify labels you typically associate with yourself in your professional and personal life. Then, challenge each of these labels by stating "I am not [label]," actively questioning the influence and permanence of these identities. I use air quotes around each label, to encourage my brain to play along.

This exercise encourages a deeper exploration of self-perception, prompting you to break free from potentially limiting labels and explore broader aspects of your identity, aiding in personal and leadership development.

- *Engage your team in a future identity time capsule exercise.* Create a time capsule focusing on your organization's evolving identity. First, document its past and current identities, reflecting on key changes and milestones. Then, encourage your team members to envision and describe potential future identities the organization might adopt in the next 50 years. Seal these reflections in the time capsule, setting a future date for its reopening. This activity fosters long-term strategic thinking and a deeper understanding of the organization's potential growth and evolution.

- *Host a 'Crucible Storytelling' dinner where each team member shares a significant event from their life that fundamentally shaped who they are today.* These stories often represent pivotal moments of challenge, change, or transformation. Encourage empathetic listening, focusing on how these defining moments cater to continuous growth and evolving identity. This activity fosters deep connections within the team and sheds light on the ongoing journey of self-discovery that is central to the trait of Continual Rebirth.

Boundless Ideation

As the years shape our minds, midlife unveils the unexpected gift: a surprising burst of creative insights.

This Midlife Leadership Superpower is marked by an exceptional blend of analytical and creative thinking, nurtured by the brain's increased bilateral coordination and matured perspective, resulting in diverse and innovative ideas.

Boundless Ideation is about harnessing midlife's enhanced cognitive abilities for strategic innovation and operational excellence. Leaders skilled in Boundless Ideation don't just encourage idea-sharing; they strategically channel these ideas into actionable strategies and initiatives.

These leaders create ecosystems within their organizations where teams are encouraged to generate ideas as well as to evaluate, refine, and implement them. They balance the environment with creativity and pragmatism, so that ideas are aligned with the strategic goals.

In this context, Boundless Ideation identifies opportunities for innovation within the organization's existing structures and processes. Leaders might introduce systems that allow for rapid prototyping of ideas, or they might establish cross-departmental task forces dedicated to exploring innovative solutions to business challenges.

Such leaders also know the importance of aligning innovation with customer needs and market trends. They employ methods like design thinking, which involves empathizing with customers, defining problems, ideating solutions, prototyping, and testing.

Secret Saboteurs — Subtle barriers to developing this superpower:

- "Venturing outside my area of expertise or established ways of thinking might undermine my authority or lead to mistakes." This reflects a fear that embracing new, possibly untested ideas or methods could be seen as risky or unwise, potentially diminishing a leader's credibility. What new perspectives could you gain by stepping beyond your current expertise, and how might these enhance your leadership? Recall a time when someone else's idea, outside their main area of expertise, led to a successful outcome. What can you learn from this?

- "Encouraging too much creative thinking might lead to unrealistic expectations and unmanageable projects." This suggests a concern that prioritizing creative over analytical thinking could result in impractical or unachievable goals, causing disruption or inefficiency. Imagine a scenario where a seemingly unrealistic idea sparked a breakthrough. What processes could you establish to harness creative thinking without losing sight of practical constraints? What balance can you strike between encouraging wild ideas and maintaining achievable goals? How might this balance differ across projects or teams?

- "If I push for too much inter-departmental collaboration, it might lead to conflicts or slow down decision-making." This implies a fear that increasing cross-functional collaboration could create tension or inefficiencies due to differing viewpoints or priorities. Can you think of a situation where cross-functional collaboration unveiled unique solutions that wouldn't have been discovered in silos? What strategies might you employ to ensure that inter-departmental collaboration is efficient and conflict-free?

Practical exercises to develop 'Boundless Ideation':

- *Establish a cross-functional innovation lab.* This serves as a dedicated space for team members from different departments to collaborate on developing and launching groundbreaking projects. Grant the team the authority to explore, create, and implement bold ideas that challenge existing norms. Include an incentive program to align individuals with the success of cross-functional and cross-departmental innovative projects.

- *Create a 'Blue Sky Thinking Space' for serendipitous conversations.* Dedicate an area in your organization as a melting pot of diverse thoughts, where serendipity leads to groundbreaking ideas and collaborations. Encourage unexpected interactions and free-flowing discussions across departments. Use thematic prompts, interactive games, and cross-functional events. Incorporate elements like idea showcases, guest speaker sessions, and creative workshops.

- *Cultivate a neurodiverse work environment.* Actively hire and support individuals with diverse neurological experiences, such as ADHD, autism spectrum, dyslexia, and others. Encourage collaboration and learning among neurodiverse teams to leverage their unique perspectives. This not only enriches the workplace culture but also broadens cognitive approaches, fostering a more adaptable mindset.

Total Ownership

Midlife opens our eyes wider, helping us see beyond just 'me' and embracing the vast world of 'us'.

Total Ownership inspires leaders to transcend individual roles, fostering a sense of collective responsibility and success through a deep appreciation of interconnectedness.

Erik Erikson's human developmental theory, particularly the stage occurring between forty and sixty-five years, aligns closely with this concept. This stage is characterized by a shift from personal achievements to contributions that benefit future generations, be it through parenting or community involvement. Successfully navigating this stage engenders a sense of accomplishment and a broader sense of ownership, mirroring a transition towards a more holistic perspective on leadership.

I also find the cultural element to Total Ownership fascinating. Shinobu Kitayama, a psychologist at the University of Michigan, found that people in rice-growing cultures — where cultivation requires high cooperation to maintain complex, shared water management systems — display collectivist tendencies, where the community's well-being is prioritized, and decisions are made collectively. In contrast, people in wheat-growing cultures, such as Japan's northernmost island of Hokkaido, tend to place a higher value than Japanese from rice-growing islands on independence and personal achievement, and are less concerned about the views of others.

Our modern, highly interconnected world is shifting these paradigms. It's becoming harder to pretend we are independent and disconnected masters of our own destiny, when global challenges demonstrate how interdependent we are. We're all becoming rice farmers.

Today's leaders of various backgrounds recognize the need for environments where team members can think and act as stewards of the entire organization, not just their individual roles. We're not just becoming rice farmers; we're effectively learning to blend traits from both rice and wheat farming cultures.

Secret Saboteurs — Subtle barriers to developing this superpower:

- "If I encourage too much ownership beyond individual roles, it might lead to overreach, confusion, or stepping on each other's toes." This reflects a fear that promoting broad ownership could disrupt established roles and hierarchies, leading to inefficiencies or conflicts. How can encouraging broader ownership enhance collaboration without diminishing clarity in roles and responsibilities? What creative strategies could you implement to ensure that every team member feels empowered to take ownership, while still respecting the unique contributions of others?

- "Taking on more than my designated responsibilities might dilute my focus and effectiveness in my primary role." This suggests a concern that expanding the scope of ownership might lead to a loss of focus or diminished performance in one's core responsibilities. Imagine a scenario where taking on broader responsibilities actually sharpens your focus and enriches your primary role. What does that scenario look like? How can fostering a mindset of 'collective achievement' rather than 'individual success' redefine effectiveness in your role and throughout the organization?

- "Instilling this total ownership mindset across all levels might be met with resistance or seen as an additional burden." This implies a fear that the shift towards a broader sense of ownership could be perceived negatively or be resisted by team members accustomed to more defined and limited roles. In what ways can demonstrating the benefits of total ownership, through concrete examples or pilot projects, reduce skepticism and encourage buy-in? What steps can you take to cultivate a culture where total ownership is embraced as an opportunity rather than viewed as an additional burden?

Practical exercises to foster a 'Total Ownership' mindset:

- *Engage in an 'I am the organization' visualization.* Regularly take time to visualize yourself as the entire organization. Complete these prompts to deepen your understanding and connection. Make up your own. I have a set of 25 cards I use with top teams. This exercise helps you to embrace the broader objectives and well-being of the entire organization.

- 'I am the organization, and I am most proud of...'
- 'I am the organization, and I succeed when we unite in...'
- 'I am the organization, and every employee should know that...'
- 'I am the organization, and I grow when we share the vision of...'
'I am the organization, and when transparency is lacking, I...'

- *Craft stories or narratives from the point of view of the organization itself.* Writing from the organization's perspective can foster a deeper emotional connection and sense of responsibility.
- *Develop an Organizational 'Alter-Ego'.* Create an alter-ego that personifies your organization's ideal traits and values. Regularly embody this persona, especially when making decisions or facing challenges. Ask yourself, "How would [Alter-Ego's Name] address this issue?" This practice encourages innovative approaches to leadership and problem-solving, embodying the essence of Total Ownership.

Timeless Impact

Come midlife, we realize our legacy isn't just what we leave behind, but how we live now, sending ripples into the future.

At its core, Timeless Impact is about creating a workplace that thrives in unforeseeable changes. It instills resilience and agility in teams and fosters a culture of continuous learning and growth. Embracing this emerging Superpower allows leaders to skillfully navigate the complexities of long-term product and market trends, guiding their organizations toward an adaptive and proactive culture. The key lies not in predicting specific future outcomes but in cultivating an organizational ethos that can endure and evolve regardless of external shifts.

Central to Timeless Impact is an understanding of the human element in leadership. It's about building legacies based on authenticity and genuine connections — reflecting structural accomplishments as well as the values, relationships, and emotions that leaders foster. This is deeply rooted in the concept of 'future self-continuity,' a principle recognized in behavioral economics and lifespan psychology. It describes how individuals align their present actions and choices with the long-term vision they have for themselves and their organization, leading to decision-making that emphasizes sustainable benefits and growth.

Leaders who embody Timeless Impact are mentors and visionaries who understand the importance of nurturing both their future selves and their organizations. They recognize that their actions today significantly shape their future trajectory, aligning their immediate decisions with a broader perspective.

Secret Saboteurs — Subtle barriers to developing this superpower:

- "Focusing too much on future impact could make me overlook current challenges and responsibilities." This reflects a fear of being so future-oriented that immediate needs are neglected. What strategies might allow you to weave your long-term vision into day-to-day operations, ensuring both immediate and future goals are met? Can you recall a leader who balanced immediate challenges with a clear vision for the future? What specific actions did they take that you could emulate?
- "Investing time in mentoring and developing others might be seen as a distraction from achieving my own career goals." This suggests a concern that prioritizing the growth of others could detract from personal achievements. What measures can you put in place to ensure that mentoring and developing others also aligns with and enhances your career trajectory? Consider the potential long-term impacts of mentoring on your organization's culture and success. How does this investment in others complement your career aspirations?
- "Shifting my leadership style to focus on long-term impacts could risk my reputation as a results-driven leader." This implies a fear that a forward-thinking approach might not align with expectations for immediate results. What examples of long-term thinking leading to significant achievements can you identify, either in your career or in the careers of leaders you admire? How can maintaining a results-driven approach while also embracing long-term vision amplify your effectiveness and legacy as a leader?

Practical exercises to develop 'Timeless Impact':

- *Envision your future self at 100.* When you're in a meditative or mindfulness state, ask yourself, "Who will I be at 100?" Even the most subtle glimpse of who you might become can develop into a North Star vision. Reflect on your values, aspirations, and legacy to align your current leadership approach with your long-term vision. This exercise encourages profound introspection, fostering personal and professional growth aligned with your core values and life goals.

- *Write a letter from your future self to your current self.* Express gratitude for the decisions and efforts you are making today. This exercise helps build a bridge between your present and future selves, fostering appreciation for your current journey and aligning your actions with your long-term aspirations and goals.

- *Practice a 'Contextual Rightness' reflection.* Engage in a mindfulness deep breathing exercise to calm the mind. Reflect on past significant decisions in a relaxed state, acknowledging the context and circumstances of each decision. Ask yourself, "Given my knowledge at the time, why was this decision right for me?" This exercise helps in embracing past choices as valuable learning experiences, essential for developing a sense of Timeless Impact.

Life Synergy

Midlife awakens a desire for authenticity, blending personal and professional lives into a journey filled with purpose.

This superpower is characterized by the intentional merging of personal life experiences and professional roles, fostering authentic and holistic growth in both spheres. Leaders become more effective at leveraging their emotional maturity and relational skills to cultivate authentic workplace cultures.

Historically, blending personal and professional experiences was generally overlooked in leadership development. In the late 1980s, Bob Eichinger and Mike Lombardo at the Center for Creative Leadership, found that 25% of senior executive learning stemmed from the personal realm, including hardships and other life lessons. As this wasn't seen as applicable to the workplace at the time, they factored 25% of the data out and focused exclusively on learning that came from on-the-job assignments, observing and working with others, and classroom lectures. In an era of blurred work-life boundaries, there are far more opportunities today to leverage personal and professional aspects combined, for greater authenticity and effectiveness.

Bill George, the Harvard Business School professor, former CEO of Medtronic, and author of the book 'True North: Discover Your Authentic Leadership,' says, "*In the past, we focused on CEO charisma, which led to command-and-control leadership. We also focused on shareholder value to a fault, which brought down many great companies. We need a different kind of leader now because let's face it: we have a lot of intersecting crises. It started with the COVID-19 pandemic and its impact on well-being, followed by supply chain shortages, millions of jobs unfilled, a threat of recession, and inflation levels we haven't seen for 40 years.*"

Leaders practicing Life Synergy understand that an organization is a collective of human beings creating value for other human beings. Shifting their focus to human connections, they embrace a more integrated approach to growth, viewing personal development as inseparable from professional advancement.

Secret Saboteurs — Subtle barriers to developing this superpower:

- "Focusing on personal well-being and connections might be seen as unprofessional or self-indulgent in a business context." This reflects a concern that prioritizing personal aspects could be misinterpreted as a lack of professionalism. Can you identify examples where personal well-being practices have directly contributed to improved decision-making or leadership presence? What steps can you take to demonstrate the professional value of personal well-being and connections, countering the perception of them being unprofessional?
- "Blending personal and professional lives could blur boundaries, leading to a loss of respect or authority." This suggests a

fear that integrating these aspects might undermine a leader's authority or professional image. Reflect on a leader you admire who successfully blends their personal and professional selves. What practices do they employ to maintain their authority while being authentic? What strategies might you develop to ensure that your authenticity strengthens rather than undermines your leadership influence?

- "Prioritizing diverse social interactions may be seen as diverting attention from critical tasks and responsibilities." This implies a concern that engaging in varied social settings could be viewed as a distraction from core duties. How could engaging in diverse social interactions enrich your leadership perspective and decision-making capabilities? Consider the potential for innovative solutions arising from diverse interactions. How can you leverage this potential without losing sight of your core duties?

Practical exercises for cultivating 'Life Synergy':

- *Integrate personal passions into your professional life.* If you're passionate about environmental sustainability and enjoy gardening, initiate a green workspace project or a corporate sustainability program. If you're an avid runner, spearhead a company-wide fitness challenge or a charity run. This action goes beyond merely balancing interests; it's about actively weaving your personal passions into the fabric of your organization's culture and goals.

- *Cultivate a culture of personal-professional integration, where team members share and celebrate their personal interests and stories.* This might involve organizing 'Passion Projects' where team members pursue initiatives inspired by their personal interests, contributing to the organization's innovation and community engagement.

- *Implement a 'Joy at Work' pulse survey Inspired by Bhutan's Happiness Index.* This survey should focus on aspects such as personal fulfillment from work projects, opportunities for using personal talents and passions, and overall workplace happiness.

From Personal Achievements
to Collective Success

Nicole faced a critical decision. One of her business unit's top fashion lines, a significant revenue generator, was suddenly thrust into controversy. A whistleblower from within Nicole's team had revealed unethical sourcing practices, causing a public outcry and a sharp decline in the larger organization's share price. This fashion line was misaligned with the company's new focus on sustainability and was slated for a gradual phase-out. Now, Nicole was under intense pressure to immediately cut the line.

She felt protective, almost maternally, towards the line her team had nurtured so diligently. But then, she remembered her soccer days and her resolution to learn to pass the ball. In a moment of clarity, she recognized that this was a moment for being generous. She needed to show generosity towards the wider company by putting the needs of the organization above her own unit's immediate interests.

She brought the issue to her team in an all-hands meeting, reminding them of the strategic misalignment, and the urgent need for action due to the whistleblower's revelation.

As the session began, Nicole was confronted with a new challenge — she noticed her team's conversation veering towards the whistleblower's identity and motives. The team's focus was not on the problem at hand but on the betrayal by one of their own. Trust within the team had been compromised, and the tensions were high. She tried to steer them back to urgent issues, but their agitation was palpable. Voices rose in frustration, and the room was charged with suspicion and resentment. The team was wasting time. Nicole felt an extreme urge to take immediate decisive action herself. At the same time, the situation required a more nuanced approach that involved managing team dynamics and emotions as much as the crisis itself. Facing this dichotomy, Nicole later told me she felt very isolated and self-doubt crept-in on her, making her question her capabilities. She wondered if she was the right person for the job, feeling the weight of leadership more acutely than ever before.

Finally, an unlikely voice cut through the tension. It was John, one of the youngest team members, typically quiet and reserved. His voice was calm yet carried a surprising weight. "My Grandma used to say, 'When someone breaks your trust, you can wait for them to mend it, or you can start weaving the threads yourself. Trust is never earned; it's always given.' She knew all about Total Ownership without the fancy words."

The room fell silent. John's words, coming from him, were unexpected. The atmosphere shifted. Nicole saw it as an opening to bring the focus back to the larger issue at hand.

Nicole stood, pacing a small circle before facing her team. Her hands gestured freely, punctuating her words, "Look, I'm in the trenches with you all. I don't have a magic answer." She stopped, locking eyes with various team members, "Sticking together when the going's good is easy. Right now? This is what tests us." She leaned on the table, closer, more personal. "We can fold, or we can make this our finest hour. What's it gonna be?"

Shifting focusing from the whistleblower, the team set out to address the problem. But first they needed to agree on what problem they were trying to solve.

The head of marketing said, "We need to renegotiate our contracts with these unethical suppliers."

The head of procurement said, "We need to address the specific design aspects of the fashion line that are tied to these unethical practices."

The website manager said, "Our customers are outraged. The problem is managing public perception and regaining customer trust."

Nicole said, "These are all very real issues. But they feel like symptoms. What's the real problem?"

The room became silent as people searched for a root cause answer.

Nicole looked at John, wondering if he had thoughts in this area that would come from a different way of thinking.

"John, your perspective on trust is quite unique," she said. "What would you say is the real problem?"

John's eyes grew big, clearly not expecting to be put on the spot. "It's the customers," he blurted out, triggering an outburst of giggles all around. John continued. "I'm serious... what I mean is... we've always focused on customers being price sensitive. Which is why we chose the suppliers we did. We became used to referring to our customers through that one label — price sensitive. And we forgot they have many labels."

Nicole nodded. "I'd like to hear more of your thoughts on lots of things," she said. "Maybe, there's a lot I can learn from you." In her mind, the idea of a reverse-mentorship program started germinating.

As ideas flowed from all corners of the room, Nicole actively listened, her eyes moving across the faces of her team, seeing their passion and commitment.

This inclusive environment sparked creativity, leading to innovative solutions and strategies that could replace the phased-out line, while aligning better with the company's direction, and an increased desire to connect with customers through many other labels.

"But it was really hard," she told me the next day, after relating the strategy meeting. "I felt like I was abandoning a part of my identity. You don't know how difficult it was to hold myself back. I desperately wanted to jump in. I felt like I was pretending to be someone else." She paused, thinking. Then she broke into a shy smile. "But you know, I actually loved watching my team play."

I could almost hear a mantra emerging, like Rajiv's: "10/10 Team Play, Everyone, Everywhere."

The Whistleblower Unveiled

Nicole inaugurated her reverse-mentorship program by formally asking John to be her mentor. During their first session, the conversation took an unexpected and transformative turn.

Nicole and John sat across from each other. John's usual quiet demeanor was replaced by a palpable restlessness. His fingers tapped on the table, and he seemed to be wrestling with an internal conflict. His eyes, usually so calm and collected, flickered with a mix of determination and anxiety.

Breaking the silence, John spoke up, his voice steady but revealing an undercurrent of nervousness. "Nicole, there's something

I need to tell you, and it's probably going to change things between us," John confessed, his voice tinged with nervous energy. "It was me—I'm the whistleblower."

Nicole's heart skipped a beat, and a wave of emotions washed over her – shock, betrayal, but also a deep sense of understanding. She had suspected it might be someone young, someone who saw the world through a different lens. "John," she began, trying to maintain a calm voice without the sharpness of anger, "I appreciate your honesty. That's part of why I started this program, to understand perspectives like yours. But, I won't lie, this is hard for me. There's a sense of betrayal, and I'm concerned about how this will affect the team's trust."

John nodded. "I know, and I'm sorry for that. I believe in transparency, and I think the team deserves to know the truth. I'm prepared for the consequences."

Nicole paused, considering his words. He had a point. "That's brave. It's going to be tough." Nicole leaned back, her mind racing. This was a test of her leadership, a moment where the values she preached were put to the test. "Let's think this through," she said slowly. "It's not just about admitting the truth. It's about how we rebuild and learn from this."

John nodded. "I understand."

But did he really? Did he grasp the gravity of the situation? The intricate web of team dynamics and trust that his admission would unravel?

Nicole gave a small, wry smile. "You've thrown me into the deep end of leadership lessons."

As they engaged in an intense, heartfelt discussion, Nicole realized this was more than a challenge; it was a moment of profound growth for both of them. Despite the initial turmoil, she felt an overwhelming sense of respect for John's integrity and courage, and a renewed commitment to guide her team through empathy and honesty.

In the weeks that followed, as John decided to leave quietly, his integrity left an indelible mark on Nicole and the company culture. His silent departure, dignified and principled, spurred Nicole to champion ethical reforms more vigorously. The experience profoundly shaped her leadership, teaching her the delicate balance between firm guidance and empathetic understanding.

For years afterward, an engraved piece of wood adorned Nicole's desk with the words, 'Trust is given, not earned; the seed of growth, not the fruit,' a constant reminder of the complex yet invaluable lessons learned from a young mentor who dared to challenge the status quo.

Nicole's Final Coaching Insights

In our final coaching session, Nicole shared her reflections. "This journey has been eye-opening but also incredibly isolating. Making decisions that could just as easily backfire as succeed feels... lonely. And dealing with John's situation, it's been a lot to process," she admitted, her gaze fixed on me, searching for answers. "You coach other CEOs. How do they cope with the isolation, the constant second-guessing? My experience with John was unexpected but invaluable. What if I'm missing more perspectives, insights from peers who've faced similar challenges?"

Our eyes met, signaling her readiness for new solutions.

"Nicole," I began, "there's a collaborative approach that you might find enriching. I sometimes facilitate a peer advisory circle, a leadership roundtable, where senior executives come together to share their challenges, experiences, and insights."

Her interest was evident. "That's exactly what I want."

And so, Nicole would soon find herself meeting Rajiv, Joanna, and Tomas.

Conclusion: From Field to Boardroom, A Journey to Mastery

Nicole's tale unraveled a crucial turning point in her professional trajectory that echoed her personal journey from high school to college soccer. By facing criticism for being incredibly competitive and lacking collaboration, she went through a pivotal transformation which was marked by the generosity to share success and responsibilities.

Nicole's story shows us that the path to midlife growth is as personal as it is professional. We need to give our vulnerabilities a chance, embrace self-awareness, and undergo personal transformations. And it is through this intertwining of personal and professional growth that we become not just better leaders but also more enriched individuals.

Chapter Three
Forging Your Executive Presence

"As a conductor
leads an orchestra,
so too,
can your executive presence
guide your team to greatness.

You're a virtuoso,
I know,
you've been a dazzling soloist,
I know,
that's what got you noticed.

And now, you'll be
a brilliant orchestra conductor."

— **Joanna Vega**

The Merger, The CEO, and
Life's Fluid Dance

Let's dive into the journey of a CEO steering their company through post-merger complexities. The CEO's aim was to build a unified team spirit where everyone felt valued and aligned with corporate goals. Yet, like many mergers, it encountered setbacks, including resistance from employees and workflow disruptions.

As the merger progressed, employees continued to follow their original company's ways of working, creating a mix of two distinct workplace cultures. To further complicate matters, a group of new hires, unfamiliar with the practices and cultures of both legacy companies, added another dynamic to the already complex cultural mix. This led to palpable tensions, manifesting in daily disagreements and a noticeable 20% increase in key staff departures. Additionally, PhoenixCorp, a major client accounting for a significant portion of the company's revenue, teetered on the brink of taking their business to a competitor.

In response, the CEO convened an urgent executive committee meeting to address and strategize a way through this escalating crisis.

Picture two different CEOs, each tackling the issue in their unique manner.

Here is the first CEO:

"Thank you for gathering at such short notice. Let's address the elephant in the room: our merger's objectives have not materialized as envisioned. We've experienced disruptions, from losing key personnel to receiving unsettling news about a major client. However, I firmly believe that if everyone here commits to the original plan and follows the strategy laid out, we can right this ship. Let's remind our teams of the importance of adhering to the new processes and unified culture we set out to establish. It's paramount that we align, streamline, and execute our strategy flawlessly. We owe it to our stakeholders and to ourselves."

Here is the second CEO:

"I want to start by acknowledging the turbulence we're experiencing. This isn't the seamless journey we anticipated, and I'm right here in the thick of it with all of you. The strains, the departures, PhoenixCorp's announcement—they're not just numbers or headlines to me. They're a call to introspection and action, starting with myself. The merger wasn't about enforcing a new culture or process; it was about creating something novel together. That's what really excited me about this merger. And I'll be the first to admit, I'm learning and adapting every day in this new reality. This isn't a journey I can—or want to—navigate alone. I need each of you. Let's set aside our old playbooks and, together, co-author this new chapter. I'm inviting an open dialogue where we share, listen, and innovate. This isn't about going back to a blueprint; it's about shaping the future together. How do we, as a collective, redefine our path forward and achieve something none of us have achieved before?"

Imagine being in the same room when each of these two CEOs addressed the issue. How did you feel and react to each one? Which CEO made you trust and want to follow them? Whose style matches your perception of good leadership?

Spotlight on the first CEO, who clearly likes structure, certainty, and control. She has a plan and gets worried about changes, feeling they could harm the company's goals. She relies on predictability and sticking to the plan. The second CEO, however, likes flexibility and working together. She sees problems as chances to think differently, collaborate, and create innovative solutions to complex problems. She's comfortable with uncertainty, believing that new ideas come from surprising places.

If you look closely at their very different leadership styles, you'll see the first CEO's need for control tends towards blaming others for problems, trying to figure out who's at fault and why. On the other hand, the second CEO looks at herself, thinking about how her own actions or lack of action might have played a part.

Consider these two approaches to leadership, seemingly opposite yet both driven by the same goal. What might surprise you is that these contrasting styles are facets of the same leader, Joanna Vega, at different points in her journey.

We met Joanna at Lake Como with Rajiv, Nicole, and Tomas. Let's go back in time to a couple years before the CEO conference at Lake Como, when I was coaching her.

In a key coaching session, Joanna tried out different leadership styles. This let her explore various sides of herself and see how she might show up for the executive committee meeting to address the merger challenges.

In the wide range of choices, like a 'sliding doors' moment, a single decision, piece of feedback, or new understanding can totally change a leader's style. This makes us wonder: How many hidden talents and unknown paths do we all have inside us? Joanna's different leadership styles show not that she's inconsistent, but that she has a wide range of skills.

Joanna shared that since she was young, she was of the thought that there was only one way she was able to lead as a CEO. That was her authentic self. She only knew and trusted a structured, predictable way. But she now realized that she didn't have to stay as her younger self. She could adopt a new leadership persona that is equally authentic.

What caused Joanna to change? What tough experience led her to find and accept a completely different way of leading?

Feedback From All Sides

When I began working with Joanna, I found that she was facing challenges in retaining her top people. Anonymous feedback from her executive committee was concerning, highlighting her lack of connection. Statements like, "I feel like I'm always on thin ice," "Joanna doesn't seem to care about us, just the numbers," and, "It's not a collaborative environment when Joanna is involved. Things have to be her way."

With the merger, Joanna faced double the responsibility and an expanded pool of executives who weren't used to her style. Their feedback, especially now, was pivotal. The combined teams were desperately seeking guidance, alignment, and, above all, understanding from their CEO. Unfortunately, many of them felt a disconnect.

In discussing ways to enhance connection with her team, Joanna began to reflect on her personal relationships. She shared a particularly personal struggle, revealing that her daughter was dealing with depression — a situation that made her question her own capacity for empathy and connection, both at home and at work.

Taking a deep breath, Joanna said, "Reflecting on the feedback I've received at work, I can't help but consider how my daughter might perceive me. What if she were to give me feedback?" She paused, looking away for a moment, her eyes glistening. "I've been so engrossed in being a CEO that I may have overlooked my most vital role at home."

She revealed that her daughter was grappling with depression. She was on medication, but she was still struggling.

"Why can't I connect with my team or my daughter? Is there something inside me that makes me a distant person? What if being a good leader and a good mother means being someone entirely different than who I've become?"

These big questions marked the beginning of a critical self-exploration at the onset of her 50s.

We often think we can separate our personal and professional lives, each with its own challenges and emotions. But we're the same person in both worlds. Our feelings, behaviors, and experiences don't exist in isolation. The challenges that emerge from the way we show up at home can appear at work, and vice versa. By making a positive change in one area, it can lead to benefits in another. Recognizing this connection is crucial for genuine growth and balance in all parts of our lives. Honestly, I think it gets harder to keep the two worlds apart as we age. When I was younger, I often wore a mask to impress others — now I just don't have the energy for that anymore.

Joanna's dilemma reflects a quintessential hallmark of midlife: the reconciliation of past achievements and identities with an emerging desire for deeper meaning and authenticity in her personal life, expecting that it will spill over into her professional sphere.

As we continued our coaching session, Joanna's insights became more pronounced. She recognized her approach at work was causing a disconnect with her team even though she was driving results, and this was because she was pondering a great deal on her relationship with her daughter. The session inspired her to try something unconventional: seeking feedback from her seventeen-year-old daughter about their relationship.

The Kitchen Conversation

When we met for our next coaching session, the story Joanna told me was both humorous and poignant.

"I sought her honest opinion," an amused Joanna recounted, "and she wittily commented, 'You're my mom, I can't rate you as a mother. But if you ask me to rate you as a cook, I'd give you a zero.'" Joanna chuckled, then her expression shifted to a thoughtful mood. "You know, her comment, though playful, got me thinking. Here I am, a CEO, not exactly fitting the traditional motherly image, and yet, there I was, slightly miffed by her jab. It's not really about my cooking, is it? It's more about this age-old expectation that as a woman, I'm supposed to be good in the kitchen." A hint of frustration laced her voice as she pondered this. "But that's beside the point, isn't it?" She smiled.

After taking a deep breath, she shared, "I decided to cook dinner myself the next evening." She paused, her face softening at the memory. "My daughter's surprise turned into participation. She stayed in the kitchen with me, and we actually talked, or rather, she talked." Joanna laughed. "Like when she was younger, on and on. It was less about the food and more about the connection, the harmony we created in that simple act."

Bringing Empathy to Work

Joanna's interaction with her daughter was a turning point in her journey, marking the onset of her transformation not only as a leader but also as an individual. She felt a new kind of ease and connection — like she was part of a team, not just leading it. This pivotal moment can be seen through the lens of **Emotional Intelligence** (EI). As Joanna navigated her personal challenges and learned to understand her emotions — as well as those of her daughter and team — she embodied the principles of EI. Her newfound ability to empathize and connect on a deeper level with her team reflects the core of EI: recognizing one's emotions and those of others to improve decision-making and relationships.

Inspired by the open communication she experienced with her daughter in the kitchen, Joanna initiated 'round-the-table' meetings at work, aiming to replicate the same level of engagement and openness, fostering a team environment where every voice could be heard.

At first, people were unsure about Joanna's new approach, but she kept at it. "I began really listening to them, taking in their ideas and weaving them into our plans together. It wasn't just about me leading anymore; we were all working in sync."

In all our sessions, Joanna talked about how things were going with her daughter. "It's like I'm suddenly seeing her in a whole new light. She's not this little kid anymore who needs me to run her life. She's becoming her own person, and what she needs from me is to listen and support. I realized I needed to let go a bit, to rethink my approach to being a mom and a boss. I'm rediscovering who I am, every day. And yeah, it feels a little daunting, but also really exciting."

As we sat in one of our last sessions, the room bathed in the afternoon light, Joanna paused, a thoughtful look crossing her face. She explained her shift in perspective, likening traditional management to Newtonian physics — with its predictable and linear methods — and contrasting it with her new approach to leadership, which she related to Quantum physics, where multiple possibilities and unpredictable outcomes reflect the complex realities of leading a diverse and dynamic team.

She leaned forward, her eyes lit with passion. "It's not just about guiding or managing; it's about influencing, inspiring, and creating spaces where innovation and transformation can spontaneously arise even within amazingly uncertain situations."

Her words hung in the air between us. Management is Newtonian. Leadership is Quantum. Joanna's insight was a testament to the profound growth and introspection unique to midlife's journey.

The Profound Impact of 'Being' Over 'Doing'

Our words and actions define us. We meticulously craft our messages, strategies, and plans — the "doing." However, a frequently overlooked, yet immensely powerful factor, is our 'way of being.' This is the presence, intent, and energy we bring to our actions.

Imagine a scenario at home. You ask your teenage child, "Have you finished your homework? I noticed you've been on your phone a lot. I want to make sure you're staying on track." Envision this statement spoken two times, using the exact same words, but in two different ways. First, from an authoritative and demanding perspective. Then, from a concerned and supportive standpoint.

While the words remain unchanged, the impact they have can vary tremendously depending on the underlying attitude or 'way of being.' The words in the statement symbolize our 'doing': our strategies, directives, and tasks. It's the tangible aspect we often prioritize. However, the tone, intent, and energy with which those words are conveyed embody our 'way of being.' It's less tangible but plays a pivotal role in how our messages are received.

You might have the perfect strategy in place, but if you fail to communicate it well by being impatient and indifferent, it might not work. Conversely, an imperfect plan delivered with genuine concern and clarity can rally people, foster trust, and achieve desired outcomes.

This concept of 'being' over 'doing' is not unique to Joanna's experience. For instance, Rajiv's journey in Chapter One demonstrates how a leader's personal demeanor can overshadow even the most meticulously crafted safety protocols. Despite the grave accidents in his factory, he was convinced of his unwavering commitment to safety, even rating it a near-perfect nine-out-of-ten. Yet, it wasn't the tangible safety processes but his 'way of being' that needed to change. Upon questioning his definition of a perfect commitment, Rajiv underwent a profound transformation. This sparked deep introspection within his leadership team about the true essence of ten-out-of-ten safety commitment.

As leaders, it's easy to get caught up in our plans and forget about the energy we bring into them. Think back to times when an interaction didn't go as expected. Could it have been the 'way of being' during that interaction that made the difference? And consider those times when, despite an imperfect plan, a positive approach made all the difference.

I often invite clients to select two or three 'being' qualities that they want to develop further. Like being adaptable, charismatic, collaborative, empowering, inspiring, among many others.

The next step is to make these concrete. Feedback is an effective way to achieve this. Ask colleagues, team members, or peers to rate you on a scale of one to ten based on your embodiment of the selected traits. You might ask, "How would you rate me as an adaptable, empowering, and inspiring leader? What would my ten out of ten look like? Have you ever seen me at a nine or a ten? What's missing, how do I get there?" The simple act of asking for such feedback can dramatically improve relationships. The feedback you receive not only offers a reality check but also gives a clear direction forward.

Understanding the importance of 'being' over 'doing' is a sign of emotional maturity, an essential part of leadership that I have often seen come into sharper focus in midlife.

Just as Joanna discovered, every leader can assess and refine their 'being' to adopt an **Authentic Leadership** style. Consider what 'being' qualities you embody in your leadership. Are you consistently genuine and heartfelt? Reflect on how enhancing these traits could transform not only your leadership style but also your team's dynamism.

Leadership's Inner Dance

Beyond guiding others, leadership is a personal journey of transformation and growth. Often for leaders in midlife, this transformation is marked by the evolving understanding of their own emotions.

As we age, our brain's prefrontal cortex, which is key to regulating emotions, develops stronger neural connections. This natural progression enhances our ability to manage feelings more effectively, a vital skill in leadership that allows for handling complex situations with calm and insight.

In this context, self-awareness becomes a key component of effective leadership, recognizing how our emotions influence our decisions and actions. Leaning into our brain's natural development during this age can enable us to respond to challenges with more thoughtfulness and empathy. We become better equipped to handle the complexities of leadership, as our emotional maturity allows us to navigate difficult situations with greater composure and insight.

Leaders who embrace this journey find themselves better able to connect with others, make more balanced decisions, and foster a positive, empowering environment. This is the essence of the 'inner dance' of leadership – a dance that becomes more nuanced and profound as we grow and evolve.

Going back to coaching Joanna, I had the privilege to witness moments of profound self-discovery. During one session, Joanna brought up a seemingly tangential concern. "One more thing," she said near the end of our session, "completely unrelated." Those last minute "one more thing" conversations are often the most important. And no, they're rarely unrelated. "How do other CEOs manage their emotions when someone underperforms?"

Was she feeling frustrated and angry? Did she frequently lose her temper? "What do you feel in those situations?" I asked.

"You know. I'm sure other CEOs feel the same thing."

Introducing her to the 'feel wheel', a visual tool that helps articulate emotions, I encouraged her to pinpoint her feelings. If you're unfamiliar with it, a feel wheel is a visual representation of a range of emotions, from basic ones at the center to more nuanced feelings radiating outward. It helps people identify and articulate specific emotions. It's a valuable tool for increasing self-awareness.

"I feel... sad, guilty, afraid, anxious. And worried. I'm disappointed in myself. Like I wasted an opportunity to be a better leader. I feel guilty that I might have given too many instructions to someone who followed my advice closely, and then didn't perform as expected. So it was my fault. I also feel a bit angry."

Our preceding conversation revolved around elevating her leadership, where she assessed herself at a seven on a scale that measured empowerment. Hoping to help her draw connections, I asked, "So, would these feelings of guilt and anxiety arise when you're lower on the empowerment scale, perhaps even less than seven?"

She slowly nodded in reflection. "Oh....," she realized, "this is all interconnected."

Joanna's admission of feelings like guilt and anxiety highlighted areas where she could improve her leadership style. Understanding these emotions allowed her to shift from merely directing her team to empowering them, aligning her approach more closely with the principles of **Transformative Leadership**.

Recognizing and understanding our emotions can unlock valuable insights and opportunities for growth. In the context of midlife, this process takes on a new dimension. As we reach this stage, we often find ourselves with a richer emotional tapestry, woven from years of experience and challenges. This depth of emotional understanding becomes a powerful tool. The real skill, however, lies in channeling these emotions, using them as catalysts to drive positive change and growth. In midlife, we are uniquely positioned to harness our matured emotional intelligence, turning it into a driving force for transformation both in our personal lives and in our leadership roles.

Joanna's journey mirrors that of many leaders who find midlife a pivotal time for self-reflection and growth. Her story serves as a catalyst for readers to examine their own emotional maturity and its impact on their leadership, encouraging a personal 'inner dance' of transformation. Transformative leaders inspire change by first undergoing personal transformation, which Joanna exemplified as she reevaluated her leadership in light of her evolving self-awareness.

Navigating Emotions for Empowered Leadership

We oscillate between a range of emotions on a daily basis, which can be broadly classified into "above the line" and "below the line." Some emotions plummet us "below the line" – a state characterized by feelings of anger, blame, despair, guilt, or victimhood, among other negative feelings. It often stems from perceiving circumstances as shaped by external forces. In such moments, we're operating under a "things happen to me" mindset.

Other emotions take us "above the line," reflecting states of assertiveness, empowerment, joy, optimism, and confidence. In this state, our creative potential is unleashed, and our ability to solve problems and trust our intuition is enhanced. This is an "I make things happen" mindset. Creativity in this state fuels our capacity to tackle complex issues with innovative solutions.

Recognizing these different states and understanding their implications is a fundamental step in cultivating self-awareness and emotional intelligence. We can examine emotions as feedback into our thought processes and beliefs. This helps us shift more easily from "below the line" to "above the line", moving from a state of victimhood, where we feel that external circumstances dictate our situation, to a state of empowerment, where we recognize and accept our responsibility in shaping our own experiences.

To make this transformation tangible and actionable, consider a three-step process:

Step one consists of recognizing when we are below the line. This involves noticing negative emotions, such as Joanna's sadness, guilt, fear, anxiety, and anger. Following that awareness, we can drill deeper, asking ourselves, "In what areas of my life am I choosing to play the victim?" This deliberately framed question compels us to acknowledge our role in maintaining a victim mindset, thereby setting the stage for transformation.

When Joanna examined this question, she found that she became frustrated with her team when their actions weren't aligned with the larger organizational goals. She blamed them for not cooperating effectively and felt defeated by the complexity of her role. In these moments, Joanna felt like a victim of the circumstances, caught in a situation that seemed beyond her control.

Step two involves taking ownership. Having identified where we feel victimized, we can then explore why we adopt this outlook. This involves understanding the paradoxical benefits of being below the line. For instance, victimhood can provide us a convenient way to sidestep accountability, to blame external factors, or to remain safely within our comfort zones. Playing the victim allows us to avoid hard truths about ourselves and can give a false sense of justification for our failures. However, this comfort comes at a heavy price, eroding credibility, respect, and trust. It hinders our ability to lead transformational change and creates obstacles to overcoming challenges. By asking ourselves, "What are the payoffs I get, and what are the prices I pay by playing victim?" we confront these uncomfortable truths.

Joanna acknowledged that her victim mindset allowed her to avoid the discomfort of the unknown. It provided a convenient excuse for not taking full responsibility for the team's disfunctions. She realized that it allowed her to maintain her existing beliefs about her role and responsibilities. However, she also understood the price she was paying: her credibility and ability to lead transformational change were at stake. "The payoffs I get and prices I pay by playing victim are avoiding change but losing trust, respect, and the opportunity to grow," she admitted.

Step Three is about taking action. Awareness and ownership pave the way for this final step. Having recognized and accepted our role in maintaining a victim mentality, we consider the potential impact of choosing responsibility instead. By adopting a proactive, empowered stance, we can transform challenges into opportunities for growth and innovation. This approach opens the door to more meaningful connections, increased trust and respect, and the ability to drive transformative change. We visualize a future where we meet challenges head-on, viewing them as chances to improve and evolve.

Joanna realised that if people weren't adopting an enterprise-wide mindset, they were likely feeling below the line, and that her own time spent in that state wasn't setting an effective example.

"By embracing responsibility together," Joanna shared, "we would really shift the way we work as a team. We would have to leave behind the blame game, and move toward a place where we all own our challenges and face them head-on, together. This way, we're not just solving problems but transforming how we see and approach our work as a collective."

I asked, "And how does it feel to say that?"

Joanna smiled. "I feel... confident, optimistic, excited even."

By going through this process, Joanna shifted from "below the line" to "above the line." She transformed her victim mindset into one of self-empowerment.

This journey from below the line to above it isn't easy, but the rewards — increased respect, credibility, and personal growth — are immense. Through the process, we become stronger and more empathetic leaders. Conscious effort to move from a state of victimhood to one of empowerment changes not only our lives but also the culture of our organizations.

Joanna's commitment to fostering a culture of understanding and collective responsibility within her team epitomizes the principles of **Servant Leadership**. By prioritizing her team's needs and focusing on their development and well-being, Joanna's transformation into a servant leader not only enhanced team dynamics but also empowered her team members to take ownership of their work and contribute more effectively to the organization's goals. Her leadership evolution from an authoritative to a servant leader model underscores the profound impact of leading by example and putting others' needs first for the greater good.

Fostering Executive Presence at all Levels

When coming out of staff meetings, Joanna began a new practice of turning to her team members and asking, "How would you rate my performance in that meeting, from 1 to 10? What could I have done differently?" The direct request initially took many by surprise. Those less experienced, accustomed to observing or taking directives in such settings, suddenly found themselves with a voice to offer feedback to their CEO.

Joanna's practice of soliciting feedback after meetings gradually reshaped the workplace culture. Team members not only grew more confident in their roles but began mirroring this behavior, creating a continuous loop of feedback that enriched interactions across all levels of our organization.

Over time, they honed their observation and feedback skills. As they were now expected to provide constructive critiques, they became more attentive during meetings, understanding not just the content but the dynamics, flow, and nuances. They had to be ready just in case someone in the meeting asked for their feedback.

Joanna's initiative reduced the impact of traditional hierarchies, cultivating a culture where open communication thrived and everyone's perspective was valued. She helped foster a culture of open communication where people felt that their perspectives mattered. As they became active in critiquing leadership behaviors, it increased their sense of accountability and ownership. This shift transformed them from observers on the sidelines to dynamic drivers of the team's success, actively shaping outcomes rather than merely witnessing them.

People felt that they were in an environment where they could be honest. Joanna was convinced that, over time, this trust would lead to more open and transparent communication across the board.

Joanna's approach didn't just affect her direct interactions. Team members were gradually emulating her behavior, seeking feedback from their higher-ups, peers, and direct reports. Feedback became part of everyday life, not just an exceptional end-of-year process.

It wasn't smooth sailing. After a particularly challenging meeting where Joanna asked for feedback, she received an anonymous message on the company's internal system: 'A leader should lead with certainty, not seek approval from her subordinates.'

In a team newsletter, Joanna addressed the anonymous critique. She wrote, 'While leadership demands decisiveness, it also benefits from humility. My aim with this feedback process is not to display uncertainty but to harness our collective intelligence. It's about ensuring that every voice, no matter the rank, contributes to our direction and decisions.'

A Ripple in Still Water

For a long time, whenever I shared the story of Joanna's moment with her daughter in the kitchen, a profound depth of emotion welled up within me, an overwhelming sense of fulfillment.

In their simple act of cooking together, I saw how our sessions had not just transformed Joanna as a leader but had also enriched her daughter's life, illustrating the extensive reach of seemingly small, personal changes.

It held up a mirror to my own emotions. Every story I hear, every transformation I witness, is a testament to the shared human journey of struggles, realizations, and growth. And in moments like these, I am reminded of why I do what I do.

From Crucibles to Catalyst

Imagine that your teenage child is struggling, and despite your many attempts, you can't seem to reach them. Their pain becomes your own, but it's a hurt you don't know how to soothe. What could you have done differently? Is it too late? The nagging sense that you are responsible is amplified every day at work when you see a similar pattern there, a pervasive aloofness that you now suspect is entirely your creation.

You stand at a crossroads between the comfort of the known and the uncertainty of uncharted paths, each choice laden with potential for personal and professional renewal. Which will you choose? This is the crucible, where your past experiences, personal pain, professional challenges, and the human aspects of leadership collide. Emotions run deep, and the promise of metamorphosis teeters on a knife-edge — your choice dictates the outcome.

You've been here before. You've faced these choices many times throughout your life. Your resilience has been growing steadily throughout your 40s, 50s, and 60s, each decade finding you more resilient than before, as we saw in the Resilience in Midlife study in chapter one.

At times, we may wish for crucible moments to pass quickly so that we can escape discomfort. But there's power in these pivotal experiences; an energy that molds our core. Every difficult decision you took, every sacrifice you made, and every challenge you've overcome has changed you, made you more resilient, and filled you with greater empathy.

Your colleagues, team, board members, clients — they, too, have weathered their own personal crucibles. Every one of them has grappled with dilemmas, made pivotal choices, and emerged renewed. Can you help others see their own crucibles and help them appreciate how past adversities transformed them?

Crucible moments strip us bare, revealing our human spirit, a boundless potential to evolve and thrive. Harnessing these stories can galvanize transformation. Treasure them, derive wisdom, and inspire others to recognize their own transformative moments.

One of my favorite retreat activities is a crucible storytelling dinner. Seated at a large round table, participants narrate events that made them who they are today. After one such dinner, a participant shared a profound insight: "Tonight, as we shared our personal stories of struggle and triumph, we saw each other not just as colleagues but as complex human beings. This mutual vulnerability transformed our group into a true team."

Enhancing Executive Presence through Midlife Leadership Superpowers

In the journey of leadership, midlife brings about a profound shift, revealing three pivotal superpowers that significantly enhance executive presence: Humility and Iron Will, Total Ownership, and Life Synergy. These superpowers are the essence of mature leadership, blending personal growth with professional excellence. As we explore these qualities, we uncover how they uniquely contribute to a leader's ability to influence, inspire, and connect at a deeper level, especially during the transformative midlife stage.

Humility and Iron Will: Leaders who balance humility with an unyielding determination project an approachable yet formidable demeanor. They are admired for their ability to listen and consider others' viewpoints while steadfastly pursuing their goals, lending them an air of approachable authority.

Picture Joanna's story not just as a tale told but as a mirror held up to your own leadership voyage. What resonated with you in Joanna's journey? Was it her bravery in embracing change, or perhaps the way she found strength in vulnerability? It's in the intersection of humility and iron will where you too will find the most authentic version of your executive presence, one that's rooted in genuine self-awareness and a natural, innate resilience to lead through change.

This is a personal journey, one that asks you to be as open to introspection as you are committed to action. It's about recognizing that the strongest leaders are those who are continually evolving, who see each challenge as an opportunity to grow, and who understand that true strength often lies in the questions we dare to ask— of ourselves, our teams, and the situations we navigate.

Total Ownership: When leaders step into the realm of Total Ownership, they transcend the traditional confines of their roles, embodying a leadership style that resonates with depth and interconnectedness. It's about recognizing that our actions ripple outwards, impacting the team, the organization, and ultimately, the broader community in profound ways, and taking conscious ownership of the ripples.

Total Ownership, particularly as it blooms in the midlife stage of leadership, enhances a leader's executive presence through the gravitas of earned wisdom and the authenticity of lived experiences. At this pivotal juncture, leaders are more adept at leveraging their accumulated insights to foster environments where collective responsibility is encouraged and celebrated. This ability to inspire shared ownership among team members—viewing success through the lens of 'we' rather than 'I'—magnifies a leader's presence. It's this unspoken generosity of commitment to the greater good that elevates their influence and commands respect.

I truly believe that Total Ownership tends to emerge naturally in midlife, as a natural evolution of a leader's journey, marked by a shift from pursuing personal accolades to seeking meaningful impact. By midlife, most leaders begin to measure success not by their individual achievements but by the growth and accomplishments of their team and the broader impact on the community and society.

Life Synergy: In the heart of midlife, the distinction between who we are in the boardroom and who we are outside it begins to blur. Life Synergy is about embracing this confluence, understanding that the richness of our personal experiences deeply enhances our professional presence and effectiveness.

Life Synergy, especially as it unfolds during midlife, acts as a catalyst for a more integrated and authentic executive presence. This stage of life encourages leaders to weave their personal passions, values, and experiences into the fabric of their leadership style, creating a presence that is both relatable and inspirational. By sharing their own stories and vulnerabilities, leaders practicing Life Synergy demonstrate that the path to professional excellence is not separate from personal growth but deeply intertwined with it. This authenticity fosters a stronger connection with their teams, enhancing trust, and encouraging a more engaged and committed workforce. It's the leader's ability to show up as their whole self that empowers others to do the same, driving innovation and creativity through a culture of openness and mutual respect.

Moreover, the natural emergence of Life Synergy in midlife reflects a leader's journey towards self-actualization, where personal and professional goals start to align more closely with one's values and sense of purpose. Leaders find themselves more adept at leveraging their life experiences to navigate challenges, inspire their teams, and make more compassionate and empathetic decisions.

In this way, Life Synergy enhances a leader's executive presence by showcasing a leadership style that is not only effective but deeply human and inherently motivating.

Conclusion: The Interwoven Journey of Leadership Evolution

Joanna's approach to leadership, enriched by her personal growth and the application of broader leadership theories, exemplifies how professional effectiveness is deeply intertwined with personal development. Her journey illuminates the impact of **Emotional Intelligence, Authentic Leadership, Transformative Leadership**, and **Servant Leadership** in creating a more empathetic, responsive, and ultimately effective leadership style. By navigating her personal challenges with introspection and empathy, Joanna not only transformed her relationship with her daughter and team but also redefined her leadership approach, underscoring the indelible link between personal evolution and professional leadership.

A pattern emerges from the stories we have explored. Whether facing workplace accidents, critical feedback, or retention issues, each leader experienced a pivotal moment that had them choose to rethink their leadership approach and look inward for solutions.

Chapter Four
Elevating Empowerment to Enterprise-wide Ownership

"Youth is wasted on the young,
they say.

Age brings wisdom,
as everyone
knows.

But the wrinkles on my face,
the aches in my bones,
make me wonder —
if wisdom is wasted on the old."

— **Tomas Ferreira**

Navigating Change with Heart and Insight

A year before the CEO forum at Lake Como, Tomas Ferreira, the 45-year-old CEO of a Lisbon-based cybersecurity firm, was wrestling with a subtle but growing issue within his team. Known for his love of personally connecting with his team members, he seized this opportunity to engage with them one-on-one, hoping to understand the underlying tensions. Through these conversations, Tomas began to notice that his team, though competent, seemed to be running autopilot, lacking the spark and innovation they once had. This was particularly disconcerting for Tomas, who had been recognized early in his career with the Eureka Innovation Award for his pioneering work in cybersecurity.

He also observed that certain areas of the business, which had expanded significantly, were not being adequately represented in major decision-making processes. This marked a significant departure from his earlier approach of running the company with an iron fist, focusing mainly on operations. Now, his emphasis on teamwork and a long-term vision was being put to the test.

To address these issues, Tomas decided to expand the executive committee from eight to ten members, aiming to bring in new perspectives and better represent the evolving landscape of the company. This strategy, inspired by a summit in Silicon Valley, reflected his recent pivot towards integrating cutting-edge technology.

Tomas hoped this expansion would foster greater inclusivity and encourage people to make decisions collaboratively. However, the dynamics evolved differently than he expected. Instead of uniting, the expanded team began forming new alliances and deepening existing divides. This left Tomas challenged in his approach and leadership as he was facing more complex team dynamics than before.

That is the point at which I began working with him. We met for our first coaching session in his office, seated together around a round mahogany conference table a few feet from his desk.

As he related the current dynamics of his team, Tomas shared several statements which astute readers might recognise as potential Secret Saboteurs.

"I like to be in the loop on key team emails, just to offer a hand if they need it."

"For certain tasks, handling them myself seems easier."

"I'm focused on maintaining our high standards for quality and consistency."

"Sometimes, stepping in early can avoid bigger issues later."

"As a leader, supporting my team through each step feels essential."

He would sometimes join meetings uninvited, 'to keep a pulse on team interactions.' Tomas shared that a nagging sense of disconnection often lingered when he wasn't directly involved in a project.

As Tomas delved deeper into the shifts happening within his team and his feelings of disconnection, his phone vibrated against the polished mahogany table, a stark reminder of the world outside this room. He glanced at it, hesitating for just a moment. He picked it up with a resigned sigh but then looked up with a hint of a smile.

"Sorry, I need to check this," he said, his tone light despite the interruption. "It's like a leash sometimes, you know? Supposed to keep you safe, but you end up just chasing your own tail."

After a brief glance at the message, Tomas chuckled softly and shook his head, setting the phone back down. "It's Alex Baumgartner from the development team. They've run into another hiccup with the rollout schedule. It's like playing Whac-A-Mole — every time you solve one problem, another pops up in its place."

I nodded, smiling at his analogy. "It sounds exhausting having to constantly keep things under control."

Tomas shrugged. "To be fair, Alex is great at what he does. He's got a knack for spotting issues before they become real problems. But," Tomas paused, his tone shifting to a more contemplative note, "sometimes I think he moves too fast for his own good. It makes me wonder if they still need me as much as I thought."

"What if you let the team play a few rounds without you stepping in?"

Tomas laughed, the sound echoing lightly around the room. "You might be onto something there. It's scary, though, like watching my teenage daughter at the wheel for the first time. You know she's capable, but that doesn't stop you from wanting to grab the steering wheel." He sighed deeply, his expression clouded with a mix of fear and resolve. "You know, it's tough watching both Elena and my team taking control and not jumping in. Maybe I'm still holding on too tightly to both."

I nodded, understanding his dilemma. "It might be helpful to see these dynamics from another angle. Have you thought about having an observer at one of your team meetings? Sometimes, watching from the sidelines could give you a new perspective."

Tomas looked thoughtful, then slowly nodded. "That's an interesting idea. Do you think it's something we could try? Having you there could provide a fresh insight into how autonomous they can truly be."

"I think it could be very beneficial," I replied. "It would allow you to see the interplay of leadership and dependency without the usual filters. It could also show you where your presence is truly needed and where it might be holding back potential growth."

He considered this, then gave a small, decisive nod. "Let's arrange for you to observe our next strategic planning session. It might just be what I need to understand how to better support their growth without overstepping."

This plan settled between us, his gaze then drifted to a picture on his desk, showing him and his daughter, Elena, laughing together on a ski trip. He picked it up and turned it toward me, a warm smile spreading across his face. "This was after she'd made it down the slope without crashing."

Recalling a personal conversation from earlier, I said, "It's almost like watching Elena prepare for her university abroad. Both at home and work, you're seeing things move forward in ways you can't control."

Tomas paused, his eyes lingering on a distant point before snapping back to the present. "That's an interesting way to put it," he said. "I hadn't thought about it like that, but you're right. There's this sense of... parting, in both places."

"Does it feel like you're losing something?" I asked cautiously, noting the softening around his eyes.

"Yeah, it does," he said, his voice quieter. "With Elena, it's obvious. But with the team... it's like I'm stepping back from something that was once entirely mine. And honestly, I sometimes miss being that person they go to for critical issues. It's a hard habit to break, feeling essential in that way." He paused and smiled at me, a bit shyly. "Maybe I actually enjoy playing Whac-A-Mole. Maybe more than I should."

Tomas related a pivotal moment with his daughter. "When Elena made her college decision," he said, "she didn't need my advice — just my trust. Looking me directly in the eyes, she asked for belief, not guidance. That moment of simple honesty made me see that my team, too, needed that same trust to thrive."

"Those are big shifts," I said. "It's natural for such changes to influence us subconsciously, maybe even in how we make decisions at work."

"It's a strange feeling, stepping back," he said. "I feel less essential in the day-to-day, which is unsettling but also liberating in a way I hadn't anticipated."

I nodded.

"And I keep thinking about..." Tomas trailed off, staring at the floor. "You know, with all the traveling I've done for work, I've missed out on a lot. And now, with Elena leaving for university, it's hitting me – all those missed moments."

Tomas' gaze drifted off as he spoke, reflecting a turmoil I hadn't seen in him before. "I've always told myself those long hours at the office were for their benefit," he murmured, almost to himself. Then, with a sigh that seemed to carry the weight of his reflections, he added, "But what if I was just... escaping?"

In that silence, the depth of his regret was palpable. I resisted the urge to fill the void with words, allowing him the space to process.

"You know, it's funny," Tomas continued after a moment, "I've always seen my work as the one place where I'm in complete control. And maybe, with everything changing at home, I've been trying to hold on even tighter at work." He sighed deeply.

I paused, letting the weight of his admission sink in. It was important to give him the space to feel heard and understood without rushing to fill the silence with platitudes. This moment was pivotal, and my role was to guide him through this introspection with care.

I nodded slowly, acknowledging his struggle, before responding.

"The realization that things are shifting, both at home and work, as a CEO and as a father, is a tough one," I said. "But it's also a chance for growth."

He looked at me surprised, then he broke into a faint smile. "I guess I've never seen it quite like that. Now the big question is, what do I do about it?"

I nodded, understanding that he wasn't really expecting an answer. Instead, his words lingered in the air, marking a poignant moment of self-awareness and vulnerability. This was not just a leader speaking but a father, a person grappling with the changing tides of life and leadership.

As we concluded our session, Tomas's reflections on his dual roles as a leader and a parent stayed with me. It struck me how often those two worlds overlap and change with time, each demanding a unique yet remarkably similar skill set. This synergy, sometimes seamless and other times fraught with tension, brought to mind the broader theme of the emotional complexities that define leadership and parenting alike.

The Leadership-Parenting Paradox

When I was a CEO, I occasionally caught myself calling team members by my teenage children's names. This curious slip of the tongue seemed to echo a deeper connection in my mind, aligning the demands of leadership and parenting into a single, intertwined challenge. I came to think of these moments as "emotional echoes," where intense feelings from one area of life reverberate into another, revealing the porous boundaries between our personal and professional worlds.

In human experience, two roles distinctly stand out for their transformative impact: parenting and leadership. As a CEO, you're accountable for your team's direction and well-being, just as you are for your children at home. This can blur lines between the two roles.

Many leaders who are appreciated by their teams, exhibit a parental energy where they are nurturing trust and guidance. This approach can create a supportive workspace, though it comes with potential pitfalls.

I've frequently observed how leaders' styles can mirror the phases of their children's lives. Those with younger children might lean towards a more controlling style, perhaps mirroring their parenting approach at home where boundaries are more pronounced. As their children grow up, the same people often develop a collaborative approach, reflecting their personal transition towards granting more independence. Over time, as our children grow and our interactions with them evolve, so too does our approach to leadership. This parallel growth illustrates our capacity for change and adaptation.

These are tendencies; not fixed rules. Obviously, every leader's approach is nuanced and influenced by multiple factors beyond just their parental role. Yet, those emotional echoes can be persistent.

For instance, a manager, who is a mother of two teenagers, often kept information close and showed visible irritation when her employees questioned her decisions. This echoed her home dynamics, where questioning could be frequent and intense. Another leader, adjusting to his team working remotely, found himself monitoring their activities closely, mirroring his concerns about his teenagers taking advantage of newfound freedoms.

A particularly telling incident occurred when a CEO, in a moment of frustration, exclaimed, "Why do they act like children?" This slip revealed not only his view of his team but also prompted a deeper reflection on how he perceived and interacted with adults both at work and at home. Our discussion about treating his team as capable adults was transformative for him, highlighting the potential for growth and change.

Recognizing these emotional echoes not only deepens our understanding of how intertwined our personal and professional lives are, but also underscores the flexibility and adaptability inherent in our roles. Statements like, "This is the decision we're going with," or "Just because our competitors are doing it doesn't mean it's the best move for us," draw from a reservoir of parental instincts applied in leadership contexts.

Our lives are woven with these intertwined threads, where emotional echoes are a natural part of our development. Leaders learn to differentiate their parental energy from their professional demeanor, gaining awareness and insight into their own growth patterns. Even for those without children, relationships with family, mentors, or roles in community settings can evoke similar emotional resonances, influencing leadership styles in profound ways.

Leaders without children also bring rich, varied experiences into their leadership styles. Whether through relationships with family and friends, mentoring roles, or community involvement, they gather unique insights that shape their approach to leadership. Like Nicole, who we saw reminiscing about missed opportunities with her now grown stepchildren.

It's crucial to acknowledge that while parenthood and leadership offer valuable lessons, each leader's journey is distinct. For Tomas, this journey had been significantly shaped by his deep-seated need to be needed — a trait that has been both a driver and a challenge throughout his leadership. This need manifested in his desire to maintain control and be the pivotal figure in decision-making, mirroring the protective and guiding role he played in his daughter's life.

As Tomas tried to embrace a less controlling, more empowering style, his underlying reluctance to fully relinquish control continued to surface, especially under pressure. This lingering attachment to being central to his team's operations not only reflected his personal struggles but also set the stage for a crisis where his resolve would be tested.

Trust and Autonomy versus Needing to be Needed

Tomas received a chilling email about a major data security breach just hours before a crucial investor meeting. Recognizing the opportunity to gain a new perspective on his team's dynamics and his own leadership, he decided to bring me in as an observer to the unfolding situation. "Seeing things from a new angle," he said on the phone, "might just show me where I truly need to be involved and where I can let go." He explained how this crisis could be a turning point — not just in addressing the immediate issue but in how he fundamentally engaged with his team. He saw an opportunity to embed trust and autonomy more deeply into his management style. Despite the instinctual tug to direct every action, he was committed to restraining himself.

I quietly entered the situation room, nodding at Tomas who briefly acknowledged me before turning his attention back to the team. The air was thick with tension and urgency. Murmurs, accusatory looks, and frantic typing underscored the gravity of the situation.

Choosing this moment to test a new approach, Tomas gathered the team's attention and wrote on the whiteboard: "How do we fix this now?" He then took a step back and announced clearly, "Alex will lead our response today. Let's give him our full support and see how we can all contribute." With this, Tomas signaled his trust in Alex and the team's capabilities despite his reservations about relinquishing control at such a critical juncture. The team, initially hesitant and accustomed to Tomas's direct style, looked between Tomas and Alex, slowly adjusting to the new dynamics set before them.

Alex stepped up, visibly energized. He quickly began delegating tasks, outlining a decentralized decision-making process. His style was methodical yet brisk.

"Let's break this down," Alex said. "We'll handle communications, technical assessments, and client outreach simultaneously. Sarah, you'll oversee the communications with our clients to keep them reassured. Michael, I need you on the technical review, assess the breach's impact immediately. And I'll coordinate directly with the response team to ensure we're proactive across all fronts."

In a bold and somewhat controversial decision, Alex decided to integrate a newly developed AI tool for crisis management. This tool, lauded for its potential in simulations, had not yet been tested under the pressures of a real-world event. Alex, however, was convinced of its capabilities. The team, though initially skeptical, nodded as the AI interface lit up their screens with data and potential action points.

However, as the AI began to operate, it was clear that the real-world application was not as seamless as expected. The tool struggled to adapt to the unpredictability of the situation, occasionally offering solutions that were either delayed or out of sync with the rapidly evolving needs of the crisis.

Tomas, leaning against the back wall, observed quietly as the team navigated the crisis. His usual command of the room was replaced by a watchful stillness. While he intended to empower Alex, his mere presence—stoic and imposing—seemed to cast a larger shadow than he anticipated. Team members, caught in a moment of indecision, would glance his way, their eyes searching for that familiar nod of approval or a guiding hand, subtly disrupting the flow of autonomy that Alex was desperately trying to instill.

The room was charged with a tension, a palpable mix of old reliance and new directives. Alex, normally resolute, hesitated more than once, his eyes inadvertently meeting Tomas's before he caught himself and redirected his focus to the task at hand.

I leaned closer to Tomas, my voice low. "Notice how the team still pivots around you," I murmured. "It's like they're spokes on a wheel with you as the hub, even now when you're trying to step back."

As the AI tool began to falter, increasing the tension in the room, the team's hesitation grew palpable, their occasional glances in Tomas's direction turning more frequent as the crisis deepened. With each misstep and error displayed on the screen, the air grew thicker with uncertainty.

Unable to remain a bystander as the situation unraveled, Tomas pushed himself off the wall where he had been leaning, his posture straightening as he took a few deliberate steps towards the center of the room. His movement alone seemed to draw the room's energy towards him.

Clearing his throat slightly, Tomas's voice cut through the murmur of disjointed conversations, capturing the team's full attention. "What are our alternatives if the AI continues to underperform?" he asked pointedly, shifting the team's focus from the faltering technology to potential solutions.

The team scrambled, pulling up backup protocols and manual override options, but the pace of the unfolding crisis outstripped their efforts to contain it. With each passing minute, the complexity of the problem deepened, and the window for an effective solution narrowed sharply.

Tomas had to proceed with the investor meeting as planned, disclosing the breach to a key shareholder. The revelation was met with immediate concern. The shareholder questioned the team's preparedness and the efficacy of their leadership in crisis situations. The meeting ended with a stern warning: ensure robust security measures and recover investor confidence swiftly, or risk a reevaluation of their investment stance.

Feeling the sting of failure, Tomas questioned his decision to step back at such a critical moment. The team's plan had failed to prevent the fallout, and now they faced the monumental task of rebuilding trust not just with their clients but also with their investors.

The following morning, I met Tomas in his office to debrief the event. By then, the immediate crisis had been contained, and systems were operational again. Tomas shared his conviction that the team was not ready for autonomy, and his closely involved leadership style was, in his view, vindicated. He believed this crisis underscored his indispensable role in the organization. Seeking my perspective, he asked, "What do you think?"

"When your team kept looking to you, it seemed they were responding more to the environment you've cultivated rather than necessity," I observed.

Tomas, turning to gaze out his office window, absorbed this.

"Last night was filled with too much guilt," he admitted after a pause. His tone carried a mix of introspection and unease. "And what you just said... it resonates more than I expected."

He then mentioned Rajiv. I had introduced Tomas to Rajiv, Nicole and Joanna, and knew that they were meeting occasionally. "Rajiv's story was on my mind all night," Tomas disclosed. He recounted how Rajiv transformed from a detached leader to one deeply connected with his team, embracing his vulnerabilities to effect real change in the face of crises — something Tomas now found profoundly relevant.

"This reflection makes me realize," Tomas continued, his voice steadying, "that my leadership needs a more personal touch. It's not just about oversight but about forging genuine connections.

The Human Executive

Tomas Ferreira's leadership evolution is a vivid illustration of the principles espoused by Brené Brown in "Daring Greatly" and "Dare to Lead," where vulnerability emerges as a cornerstone of effective leadership. This approach is validated by Amy C. Edmondson's concept of psychological safety from "The Fearless Organization," which advocates for environments that promote risk-taking and innovation without fear of negative consequences.

During the crisis meeting, Tomas demonstrated his evolving approach by asking, "How do we fix this now?" His reflection the following day marked a significant shift from seeing the event as a need for control to recognizing his role in fostering a restrictive environment.

This growth was further emphasized during a retreat I facilitated for Tomas and his executive team. We introduced an exercise where leaders were to respond with "I don't know" to every question, simulating a scenario of embracing uncertainty. Initially met with discomfort, the exercise gradually revealed its value as Tomas encouraged openness. A board member who came to speak at the retreat dinner shared a powerful insight, stating, "Acknowledging our limitations does not undermine our authority but rather humanizes us, fostering a culture where learning and innovation can flourish."

Beyond Boundaries with Tomas's Vision of Enterprise Unity

During the retreat, we discussed what empowerment really means — moving beyond just assigning tasks to truly delegating authority, allowing the team not just to start projects but also to carry them to completion without constant oversight. Tomas devised a scale he could use for feedback, to understand how others perceive his level of empowerment, from one to ten, where one meant delegating tasks and ten meant delegating authority.

Feedback from his team varied. One senior manager said, "At

the beginning of a project, you're incredible at setting the vision and giving us the autonomy to execute — I'd rate that an eight on the empowerment scale. But as we dive into the execution phase, you become increasingly hands-on, checking in daily, sometimes offering unsolicited solutions. That feels more like a two or three. It's as if you trust us to start, but not necessarily to finish."

An unexpected piece of feedback from a newer team member was particularly eye-opening: "There seems to be a 'right way' to communicate, a sort of unspoken 'Tomas-language.' If I don't phrase things a certain way or present in a particular style, I feel my ideas aren't as well-received."

At the end of the retreat, Tomas shared, "I used to believe that empowerment was about giving more responsibilities to others. But I've learned it's about taking away the barriers that get in the way."

I asked, "What do you mean by barriers?"

"I may have inadvertently set up these walls, making my team adapt to 'Tomas's way'. Empowerment is about dissolving those barriers and giving everyone the space to bring their unique strengths, perspectives, and methods to the table. It's not just about tasks or authority; it's about creating a space where everyone can thrive authentically."

Tomas's story is a testament to the ongoing nature of midlife transformation. His journey — marked by introspection, shifts in leadership style, and implementing a culture of empowerment — mirrors the dynamic process of growth characteristic of this life stage. This phase of life offers leaders like Tomas an unparalleled opportunity to redefine the very fabric of their organizations.

The Midlife Cognitive Shift in Leadership

Tomas, now referring to his role as that of a Change Catalyst, showcases a midlife cognitive shift from the agility of fluid intelligence, marked by quick, innovative thinking, to the strategic use of crystallized intelligence, which represents a wealth of knowledge, life experiences, and insights into human behavior, communication, and conflict resolution. This rich repository enhances his ability to drive meaningful change.

However, this shift can be emotionally complex. For Tomas, adapting to this new cognitive style brought mixed emotions. He sometimes missed the spontaneity and quick adaptability of his younger years, grappling with a sense of nostalgia. Acknowledging and mourning these changes was a complex emotional journey, crucial for reconciling with his evolving professional identity.

In his role as a Change Catalyst, Tomas now exemplifies several key identities. He is a Collaborative Innovator, bringing together diverse viewpoints to forge new solutions, and an Ethical Steward, upholding integrity from a career's worth of ethical decision-making. Each identity—from being an Inspirational Mentor to a Visionary Guide—reflects the deep wisdom, empathy, and resilience he has developed through his midlife experiences.

Tomas's emotional journey through this transition was pivotal. He experienced moments of self-doubt, questioning whether his accumulated wisdom was as valuable as the agile thinking of his younger years. But by embracing these identities, leaders like Tomas can navigate changes in cognitive abilities. This progression doesn't only leverage wisdom; it also adapts to changes in thinking and operation styles.

The next section will explore how leaders like Tomas deal with grief in midlife transformations. For Tomas, grief wasn't just about loss; it was about coming to terms with the evolution of his cognitive abilities and professional role. Accepting these changes involved deep reflection and gradually embracing a new leadership identity, which in turn enriched his ability to empathize, persevere, and inspire.

The Hidden Strength in Struggle

At Tomas's team retreat, a young team member who is usually quiet, shared her experience of caring for her terminally ill in-laws. Her story revealed challenges and resilience as she navigated the progression of dementia, the emotional toll of seeing loved ones bedridden, and ultimately their passing. A poignant detail emerged: her eight-year-old son took the initiative every morning to lay out the medication, and each afternoon after school, ensured it had been administered.

"I never knew how strong you were," Tomas remarked, with nods of agreement and admiration coming from the team. Some team members quietly wiped away tears, while others exchanged understanding glances.

This story transcended business strategy; it was about the universal human experiences of grief and resilience.

Midlife brings a depth of emotional insight for senior executives, often intertwined with grief. This stage, ripe with personal and professional re-evaluations, enhances leadership transformation:

- Navigating Leadership Succession: Dealing with the departure of trusted colleagues or mentors often involves a sense of loss. This experience provides a critical opportunity to reassess and affirm one's leadership style, adapt to new dynamics, and strengthen team cohesion.
- Managing Technological Disruptions: Adapting to industry changes requires the emotional intelligence to guide teams through uncertainty and foster a culture of continuous learning and adaptability.
- Overseeing Organizational Changes: Leading through mergers or restructuring involves addressing team anxieties and uncertainties. The resilience gained from personal grief experiences can be instrumental in understanding and empathetically managing team emotions during these transitions.
- Balancing Work-Life Integration: Managing personal health or wellness challenges, along with work responsibilities, requires a keen understanding of one's limits and capabilities, enhancing the leader's ability to empathize with team members facing similar situations.
- Reassessing Goals and Legacy: Midlife often prompts leaders to reflect on their career impact. This introspection can lead to a more focused and meaningful approach to leadership, where the emphasis shifts to legacy-building and long-term value.

By midlife, grief and loss have become profound teachers that can refine leadership qualities. This can sharpen decision-making, deepen empathy, and nurture a leadership style that is effective in guiding teams through uncertainty.

The five stages of grief, as outlined by Elisabeth Kübler-Ross, can metaphorically apply to professional transitions, offering a framework to understand emotional responses to change. While not a direct comparison, these stages—Denial, Anger, Bargaining, Depression, Acceptance—help illuminate the emotional journey leaders may undergo when faced with significant professional up-heavals.

Initially, there's Denial, where leaders might refuse to accept new challenges or changes, preferring the comfort of the status quo. Then comes Anger, characterized by frustration or blame towards others or external circumstances for any setbacks. Next is Bargaining, where leaders might try to find ways to avoid facing the full impact of the change, often through negotiations or compromises. Depression follows, often as a sense of helplessness or demotivation in response to the challenges. Finally, Acceptance is reached, a crucial stage where leaders acknowledge the new situation, learn from the experiences, and adapt their approach to move forward effectively. Understanding these stages helps navigate emotional responses to professional challenges with greater awareness.

Fostering a culture that acknowledges emotional challenges and honours the grieving process, creates an organization that can drive and respond to continuous transformation.

Fostering Enterprise-wide Ownership through Midlife Leadership Superpowers

Three Midlife Leadership Superpowers are instrumental in nurturing a culture of enterprise-wide ownership: Total Ownership, Boundless Ideation, and Timeless Impact.

Total Ownership: While Total Ownership was previously outlined as a midlife leadership superpower crucial for enhancing executive presence, its role in fostering enterprise-wide ownership involves catalyzing a shift in organizational culture.

Leaders practicing Total Ownership not only model this behavior but actively engage in developing systems and processes that encourage every team member to see the value of their work in the broader context of the organization's mission and success.

By midlife, leaders have developed a broad perspective on how individual roles contribute to the larger mission. This depth of experience enables them to develop systems and processes that encourage a culture of ownership.

This might include:

- Implementing transparent communication strategies that provide all employees with insight into how their roles contribute to the organization's objectives.
- Developing a recognition program that celebrates not just individual achievements but also team and cross-departmental successes, reinforcing the interconnectedness of all roles within the organization.

Boundless Ideation: For Boundless Ideation, the focus shifts from personal cognitive development to creating a culture that values and cultivates diverse and innovative thinking at all levels and across departments, functions, and other organizational boundaries. This superpower becomes a cornerstone for nurturing an environment where ideas flow freely, and employees feel a strong sense of ownership over the creative process and its outcomes.

The cognitive development characteristic of midlife, including enhanced bilateral coordination of the brain, allows leaders to balance creative and analytical thinking, fostering an environment where diverse, innovative ideas are encouraged and valued. Their matured thought processes allow them to see connections and possibilities that younger leaders might miss, thereby promoting a culture where creative solutions are pursued with vigor and enthusiasm.

Strategies might include:

- Establishing regular ideation sessions across all levels of the organization, ensuring that everyone, regardless of their role, feels empowered to contribute ideas.
- Creating a 'fail-forward' culture that views setbacks as essential learning opportunities, thereby encouraging risk-taking and innovation without the fear of failure.

Timeless Impact: When viewed through the lens of fostering enterprise-wide ownership, Timeless Impact involves leaders embedding a long-term vision into the organization's DNA. This superpower is about inspiring teams to work towards a legacy that transcends the immediate and tangible, encouraging a deeper sense of pride and ownership in their contributions to the organization's enduring values and impact.

Midlife leaders are at a point in their careers where they start to think more about legacy and long-term impact. They're motivated not just by immediate gains but by the desire to leave a lasting, meaningful mark, inspiring their teams to adopt a similar long-term perspective.

This can be achieved by:

- Facilitating workshops and discussions that allow employees to connect their personal values and goals with the organization's long-term vision, fostering a shared sense of purpose.
- Integrating sustainability practices and social responsibility initiatives into the organization's core operations, demonstrating a commitment to making a positive impact on society and the environment.

Conclusion: Holding On and Letting Go

Reflecting on Tomas's journey, it's clear that while he made significant strides toward a more empowering leadership style, his deep-seated need to be needed subtly lingers in the shadows of his progress. This chapter has traced moments of breakthrough alongside instances of backsliding—a dance between old habits and new insights.

Although Tomas has adopted new ways of leading, his enduring need to feel indispensable continues to cast a long shadow. This ongoing struggle does not detract from his achievements but rather highlights the complex nature of midlife transformation as a continuous balancing act between past inclinations and future aspirations.

I recognized an opportunity for my own growth as a coach. Perhaps there were depths I did not fully explore — early traumas or formative experiences that might explain Tomas's persistent behaviors, especially as such issues often re-emerge during midlife, influencing current behaviors and leadership styles. This realization spurred me to delve deeper into the impact of psychological trauma on midlife leaders. By integrating trauma-informed coaching practices, I could better understand and address the underlying emotional drivers, including those reactivated traumas from earlier life stages, thereby offering future Tomas's more empathetic and nuanced support.

Tomas's story, shared with vulnerability and introspection, offers profound lessons for other leaders facing similar transitions. It underscores the importance of acknowledging and addressing deep-seated emotional needs, not just for personal growth but also for fostering more authentic and effective leadership.

Chapter Five
Lyrical Leadership

"Traveler, your footprints
Are the path and nothing more;
Traveler, there is no path,
The path is made by walking."

— Antonio Machado

Subject: Exploring New Dimensions of Leadership at Como
From: Tomas Ferreira
To: Joanna Vega, Rajiv Mehta, Nicole Parker
Date: 13 October 2023

Dear Joanna, Rajiv, and Nicole,

I'm eagerly looking forward to the upcoming CEO forum in Como—it will be delightful to finally meet face-to-face after almost a year of insightful and inspiring virtual conversations. Our recent conversation on how the exploration, risk-taking, and identity formation of entrepreneurship (or Rajiv's intra-preneurship) defined our early careers sparked a thought-pro-voking question: What inspires us in our 40s and 50s? My unexpected answer is poetry.

Wait. Let me explain. Bear with me as I make what might seem like an unexpected leap.

Our last discussion got me thinking about how we navigate the paradoxes of a 'both-and' mindset. Joanna, your concept of this being a 'midlife leader's superpower' really resonates with me.

It turns out that poetry is fundamentally built on this skill. I've come across fascinating insights from the corporate and academic worlds.

• **"The language of poetry is the language of paradox."** — Cleanth Brooks, a pioneering figure in 20th-century literary criticism. Brooks positions poetry as an unparalleled medium for expressing intricate, complex, and conflicting truths.

• **"I used to tell my senior staff to get me poets as managers. Poets are our original systems thinkers. They look at our most complex environments and they reduce the com-**

plexity to something they begin to understand." — Audio pioneer Sidney Harman, the founder of Harman Industries.

• Satya Nadella, CEO of Microsoft, describes poetry as "that force created within us that seeks out the unimaginable, that gets us up to solve the impossible."

• **"As you rise in business, as you get out of the lower level staff jobs and the quantitative analysis, and you get into the higher level of problems, I felt that I had an enormous advantage over my colleagues because I had a background in the imagination, in language and in literature."** — Dana Gioia, Chairman of the National Endowment for the Arts, a poet who began his career at General Foods and eventually became vice president of marketing. He was a Stanford MBA graduate a few years before your time, Nicole, but perhaps you've come across his name?

• **"A poet's work is all about creating a language big enough to represent both the world you inhabit and the next, larger world that awaits you."** — David Whyte, a poet who's walked the halls of Astra-Zeneca, Boeing, Citigroup, and more, showing them how poetry can open up new ways of thinking.

I've also read intriguing fMRI studies, all very recent discoveries that shed light on poetry's impact on cognitive and emotional skills. It's quite interesting how this aligns with our leadership experiences. Have any of you encountered this in your reading or reflections? I included references for the detail-lovers among us (**looking at you, Joanna**).

• **Engaging with poetry activates brain areas associated with managing uncertainty and refining complex thought processes** ('Shall I compare thee: The neural basis of literary awareness and its benefits to cognition' by O'Sullivan et al., University of Liverpool, 2020).

• **Composing poetry strengthens language and executive control networks, fostering cognitive flexibility and connectivity, which significantly boosts problem-solving and innovation abilities** ('The impact of knowledge on poetry composition' by Ruizhi et al., Brain and Language, 2022).

• Poetry activates introspection and emotional response centers, particularly in the right hemisphere, enhancing emotional intelligence and empathy — **key components of the changes we've been noticing in our own growth as leaders** ('What's the Relationship Between Poetry and the Brain?' Exploring Your Mind, 2020).

• **You're a poet and you didn't know it!** Researchers observed a distinctive burst of electrical activity in non-expert subjects' brains that occurred in the fraction of a second after hearing the last word of a poetic line, suggesting we are innately wired for poetry ('Implicit Detection of Poetic Harmony by the Naïve Brain' by Vaughan-Evans et al., UK's Bangor University, 2016).

I wonder if any of you have experienced moments where poetry or similar reflective practices have offered clarity or a new perspective on leadership? This got me thinking, what if we tried a small experiment for our next meeting, as a way to share and delve deeper into these experiences?

We can each bring a poem that deeply resonates with us, personally or professionally. Or, if you're feeling inspired, try your hand at writing a few verses of your own. It doesn't have to be polished or profound—just something that captures a glimpse of your leadership journey or philosophy. This could be fascinating! Imagine the new dimensions we'll uncover in our leadership—and ourselves—through the lens of poetry.

What do you say? Are you game? Are we ready to discover the poets among us?

Looking forward to seeing where this journey takes us. I can't wait to hear your thoughts and see the poetry you resonate with—or the verses you're inspired to write.

Warm regards,
Tomas

Subject: Sharing My Reflection - "The Chase"
From: Tomas Ferreira
To: Joanna Vega, Rajiv Mehta, Nicole Parker
Date: 15 October 2023

Dear Team,

Nicole just called me and suggested I kick things off. So, here is my poem, "The Chase." It explores the paradox of chasing wisdom in youth and longing for youthfulness in wisdom. Here it is:

The Chase
Youth is wasted on the young,
they say.
Age brings wisdom,
as everyone
knows.
But the wrinkles on my face,
the aches in my bones,
make me wonder —
if wisdom is wasted on the old.
I have chased after wisdom while young,
and youthfulness when old.
And sometimes,

in stillness,
I catch them both.

This piece reflects my journey of seeking balance between ambition and mindfulness. Curious to hear your thoughts and any reflections it might inspire in you.

Best,
Tomas

Subject: RE: Sharing My Reflection - "The Chase"
From: Rajiv Mehta
To: Tomas Ferreira, Joanna Vega, Nicole Parker
Date: 15 October 2023

Dear Tomas,

Your poem "The Chase" struck a deep chord with me. The paradox of seeking both wisdom and youthfulness is poignant.

I have to admit though, I'm wrestling with a thought — I'm worried about leaning too much into reflection and vulnerability that we might risk blurring the assertiveness expected of us. How do we ensure that this level of introspection doesn't overshadow the confidence and decisiveness crucial to our roles? Curious to hear your views on finding that equilibrium.

Thank you for sharing such a personal piece.

Warm regards,
Rajiv

Subject: RE: Sharing My Reflection - "The Chase"
From: Nicole Parker
To: Tomas Ferreira, Joanna Vega, Rajiv Mehta
Date: 16 October 2023

All,

I'm moved by the vulnerability in Tomas's poem shared. I'm excited and inspired to reflect on the masks we wear, and the liberation found in authenticity. Here's my attempt to capture that journey. I was inspired by Rudyard Kipling's poem, "If". But I wanted to reframe it more forcefully, as in "not if, but when."

WHEN we laugh and play
with our many identities,
when we see that all of these
are masks,
when we let go
of outdated labels
even if we still love them
very much,
then,
our genuine, authentic self
can shine through,
more complex,
more beautiful,
than any label
could possibly capture.

WHEN we let go of old dreams
that we still love dearly,
when we celebrate
our successes and failures equally,
when we laugh
at the limiting beliefs

that cause us to screw up
magnificently,
then,
we can live joyfully,
in the present moment,
perform at our
very best,
with our results and our words
in alignment.

WHEN we let go of
our expertise and authority,
when we pretend to be
junior apprentices again,
when we allow ourselves
to act like children
in spite of years of
experience,
then,
we can enjoy the thrill
of being a beginner,
embark on new journeys,
and fulfill our purpose
of bringing new creations
into the world.

More than all of this,
we can discover
that our nature is to thrive
and live most fully,
in times of change,
uncertainty
and ambiguity.

Eager to know if this strikes a chord with any of you.
Warmly,
Nicole

Subject: RE: Sharing My Reflection - "The Chase"
From: Joanna Vega
To: Tomas Ferreira, Rajiv Mehta, Nicole Parker
Date: 17 October 2023

Tomas and Nicole — you're very creative!

Diving into the scientific research Tomas shared, I was struck by how the studies on poetry's impact on the brain illuminate the very paradoxes you both have captured in your poetry. Tomas, your portrayal of the perpetual dance between wisdom and youth, and Nicole, your depiction of the journey towards authenticity beyond our professional facades, both resonate deeply with the cognitive and emotional duality highlighted in the literature.

This fusion of creativity with pragmatism inspired me to reflect on our roles as leaders. We navigate between decisiveness and openness, strength and vulnerability, echoing the brain's dual engagement with poetry. Perhaps, then, the essence of leadership lies in our ability to hold these tensions in a productive balance.

Here's my attempt to thread this understanding into verse. I needed help from a friend, so I kind of cheated, but only a little bit.

The Executive Presence of a Maestro
As a conductor
leads an orchestra,
so too,
can your executive presence
guide your team to greatness.

You're a virtuoso,
I know,
you've been a dazzling soloist,
I know,
that's what got you noticed.

And now, you'll be
a brilliant orchestra conductor.

Your unique gifts,
your music, my friend,
will now inspire, and touch,
many hearts, through instruments
played by others.

Each beat of your baton,
the smallest nod of your head,
a gentle smile, a gesture so slight,
guides your team to their peak,
every instrument in perfect harmony.

Your team will play flawlessly,
I am certain, thanks to your presence.

The time is now,
so step out, my friend,
into the spotlight,
and let your presence guide the way,
through the performance of a lifetime.

It symbolizes my evolving understanding of leadership.
Thoughts?

Best,
Joanna

Subject: RE: Sharing My Reflection - "The Chase"
From: Joanna Vega
To: Tomas Ferreira, Rajiv Mehta, Nicole Parker
Date: 17 October 2023

I forgot to add this — I found something very interesting in the links Tomas shared. A real gem. Did you know that in ancient Greek, being a poet meant you were 'a maker'?

This concept really resonated with me, especially when considering leadership. It's about envisioning what could be and then dedicating ourselves to bringing that vision to life.

Just as poets craft and refine their verses, leaders shape and adjust their strategies and teams to achieve a harmonious outcome.

This process of creation and iteration, rooted in the ancient meaning of poetry, or 'Poesis', highlights that leadership, at its core, is a poetic act—transforming vision into reality.

Sincerely,
Joanna

Subject: RE: Sharing My Reflection - "The Chase"
From: Tomas Ferreira
To: Joanna Vega, Nicole Parker, Rajiv Mehta
Date: 21 October 2023

I love that, Joanna. I can't see how it would be possible to be an effective leader, especially one able to inspire others with a vision of success, without having a deeply creative imagination.

Subject: Re: Nicole and Joanna's Poetic Insights
From: Rajiv Mehta
To: Tomas Ferreira, Joanna Vega, Nicole Parker
Date: 17 October 2023

Dear Tomas, Nicole, and Joanna,

I've been genuinely moved by the poetry you've shared.
Each of your poems has touched me, reminding me of the
rich, layered experiences that form our leadership journeys.
Joanna, I'm still digesting what you said: "Perhaps, then, the
essence of leadership lies in our ability to hold these tensions
in a productive balance."

Looking forward to our continued exchange of ideas and
inspirations.

Best,
Rajiv

Subject: Rajiv's Reflections: A Glimpse into the Stillness
From: Tomas Ferreira
To: Joanna Vega, Nicole Parker, Rajiv Mehta
Date: 21 October 2023

Dear Joanna, Nicole, and Rajiv,

Moments ago, I had the pleasure of a deeply inspiring conversation with Rajiv. While he's been a bit reserved in our email
exchanges, his insights during our call were nothing short of
profound.

Rajiv, I hope you don't mind me saying, but the ideas you

shared about your poem captured a beautiful essence that I believe deserves to be shared with Joanna and Nicole. Your thoughts on navigating the complexities of leadership, the weight of expectations, and the silent spaces between our relentless pursuits were truly moving.

Rajiv eloquently spoke of the moment of stillness—not as a pause but as a rich, vibrant space where true insight and transformation can occur. It reminded me of the insightful paradoxes we've been exploring through our poetry and discussions.

With your permission, Rajiv, I'd love for you to share those budding lines you mentioned. There's a universality in your reflections that I believe will resonate deeply with all of us, shedding light on the shared yet unique paths we tread as leaders.

This journey of ours, exploring leadership through the lens of poetry, has been unexpectedly revealing. Each poem, each reflection, adds to the tapestry of our collective wisdom and experiences. Rajiv, your voice and insights are an integral part of this exploration.

Let's continue to encourage and inspire each other, delving deeper into the stillness and the storm of leadership and life.

Warmest regards,
Tomas

Subject: My Reflections in Verse
From: Rajiv Mehta
To: Tomas Ferreira, Joanna Vega, Nicole Parker
Date: 22 October 2023

Dear Tomas, Joanna, and Nicole,

Firstly, Tomas, thank you for your kind words and for our recent conversation, which indeed sparked courage within me to share more openly.

A bit of background — I aced the poetry section in my 10th-grade board exams, topping my region, but maths was a different story. Given the emphasis on practical subjects at home, I chose to focus more on maths and sciences thereafter. So I do know about poetry, more than I should.

Joanna's words inspire me to hold my own internal conflict in, hopefully, a productive balance. With a bit of hesitation still in my heart, I've decided to share the few lines I mentioned to Tomas. This poem reflects my recent journey through, the pressures we all face, and the stillness that I've found to be both a challenge and a sanctuary.

Beyond Burnout
Hard-won
knowledge,
authority,
and expertise,
rocket me skyward;
this has been my way.

But the stress
in my chest, the
restless nights, and
frayed connections, are
warnings I must heed.

My fuel is almost spent, I know,
my way will not propel me further.
With nothing to grasp for safety,
no knowledge, authority, or expertise;

I linger in the black stillness, suspended,
between ascent and descent.

In that stillness, a spark of insight —
I am alive; and I still have dreams.

So I extend my arms like open wings and
catch starlight particles to sail toward
the next stages of my life.

This poem is my attempt to articulate the liminal space between relentless pursuit and the poignant clarity that comes when we allow ourselves to pause, even if involuntarily. It's about recognizing the signs of burnout, yes, but also about finding a new direction in the vastness of uncertainty.

I hope these words resonate in some way with you, as your poems and reflections have resonated with me. Thank you for inspiring me to share, and I look forward to our continued exchanges.
Warm regards,
Rajiv

Subject: RE: My Reflections in Verse
From: Joanna Vega
To: Rajiv Mehta, Tomas Ferreira, Nicole Parker
Date: 22 October 2023

Rajiv,

Thank you for sharing such a powerful piece of your heart and journey with us. Your poem "Beyond Burnout" resonates deeply. I need to appreciate those moments of stillness and find strength in them instead of trying to transform them into action.

Thank you for this gift.
Joanna

Subject: RE: My Reflections in Verse
From: Nicole Parker
To: Rajiv Mehta, Tomas Ferreira, Joanna Vega
Date: 22 October 2023

Dear Rajiv,

"Beyond Burnout" is truly moving. It's remarkable how you've distilled such complex emotions and experiences into verse.

It's inspiring to see how each of us brings our unique voice to this shared space.

It's an honor to embark on this poetic journey alongside you.

Warmly,
Nicole

Midlife Creativity

Joanna's revelation that "poet" originally signified a creator, someone who molds and manifests the 'new' through imagination and language, clarified my own entrepreneurial journey. Building my company felt much like crafting a piece of art.

However, friends often quipped, 'That's not art. That's business.' This dismissal echoes the French term 'magouille,' which implies scheming — a common skeptical view of entrepreneurship in France. This perception fails to recognize the creative essence required to transform vision into reality.

In my work as a coach, I have often glimpsed the same creative artistry flowing out of the minds of senior executives, all of whom were — as Tomas might say — poets who perhaps didn't know it.

Many leaders recognize the artistry required in their roles. Leaders, like artists, start with a vision—often just a spark. Through strategic decisions and team dynamics, they sculpt this vision into tangible outcomes, much like an artist shapes a sculpture from clay or a composer arranges harmonies to create a symphony.

Yet, despite these parallels, few leaders would claim the title of artist. Art and business are seen as distinct realms. Business is often perceived as a domain ruled by logic and efficiency, while art is the realm of creativity and expression. This underappreciation of the artistic aspects of leadership diminishes the role of creativity and innovation in business success, fostering a limiting 'either-or' mindset. Therein lies one of the emerging paradoxes of modern leadership in a changing world, and a potential opportunity — the ability to effectively hold two opposing ideas at the same time: a results-oriented business mindset and an artist's mindset.

Embracing business and art can unlock new levels of innovation and engagement where leaders can explore uncharted territories with the confidence of a creator.

You know where this is going: midlife leaders are uniquely positioned to harness both business and artistic mindsets more effectively than in their younger years.

Supporting this artistic approach, a study by Hasher et al. (2009) suggests that the aging brain's increased distractibility might actually enhance problem-solving, offering midlife leaders an edge in blending analytical rigor with creative insight, in ways not as accessible in their younger years.

Early in one's career, the practical dismissal of seemingly frivolous pursuits like poetry is understandable. However, as leaders mature, embracing such creative expressions can become a valuable asset, unlocking deeper insights and innovation.

Fostering a Combined Business and Artistic Mindset through MidlifeLeadership Superpowers

Examining the intersection of business acumen and creativity, this section illustrates how three Midlife Leadership Superpowers — Boundless Ideation, Continual Rebirth, and Humility and Iron Will — enable senior executives to harmoniously blend analytical and artistic perspectives.

Boundless Ideation: This superpower champions a holistic approach, melding curiosity with innovation to dissolve the traditional barriers between business logic and creative processes. Curiosity is the key emotion, driving the desire to explore, learn, and innovate beyond conventional boundaries.

Midlife leaders have accumulated a vast array of experiences, from successes to failures, across various contexts and cultures. This richness provides a broader palette of ideas, perspectives, and approaches to draw upon when facing challenges. Midlife cognitive abilities enable leaders to synthesize these diverse inputs, fostering a unique blend of business acumen and creativity that is less common in earlier career stages.

A significant midlife benefit is comfort in holding contradictory thoughts and navigating paradoxes. Leaders learn that business and art, logic and creativity, strength and flexibility are not opposites but complements. This ability to embrace and leverage contradiction enhances their capacity to lead in complex, uncertain environments.

Continual Rebirth: This superpower Inspires leaders to perpetually reinvent themselves and their methods, tapping into the artistry and creativity within themselves and their organizations. It's about embracing change as a creative force, encouraging a dynamic interplay between past experiences and future possibilities. Optimism, a forward-looking emotion, characterizes this superpower, embracing change and heralding new beginnings.

The introspection and self-awareness that come with midlife equip leaders to navigate their continual rebirth with confidence and clarity. They understand the cyclical nature of growth and the value of shedding outdated identities or methods that no longer serve them. Armed with this self-knowledge, leaders apply an artist's mindset to business challenges, transforming perceived obstacles into opportunities for innovation.

Humility and Iron Will: This Superpower cultivates a mindset where leaders embrace both the pragmatism of business and the fluidity of artistic creativity. It encourages executives to remain open to being a beginner while persistently striving for innovation and excellence.

Midlife fosters a balance between confidence, grounded in years of accomplishments, and a humility that welcomes continual learning. This balance is crucial for blending the structured world of business with the fluid, exploratory nature of artistic thinking. Leaders in midlife are uniquely positioned to champion this dual mindset, driving their teams toward solutions that are both pragmatic and innovative.

Conclusion: Embrace Your
Artistic Leadership

Take a moment to look back at your own journey. Recognize the many identities you've assumed based on versions of yourself and the roles you've played. Acknowledge the resilience it took to let go and evolve each time your identity evolved. That resilience is your gift, your inherent strength. Let it inspire you to embrace change with open arms and to see every ending as the birth of a new beginning.

What change is waiting for you to embrace? What new persona is ready to emerge? Let these questions guide your journey forward. Embrace your innate resilience, step into the future, and become the leader you are meant to be.

Chapter Six
Transforming Workplaces into Thriving Communities

"It is probable that the next Buddha will not take the form of an individual. The next Buddha may take the form of a community, a community practicing understanding and loving kindness, a community practicing mindful living. This may be the most important thing we can do for the survival of the earth."

— **Thich Nhat Hanh**

Chronicles of a Corporate Renaissance

Inside the calm, minimalist virtual café, where holographic servers glided silently between tables and digital windows displayed serene, ever-changing landscapes, Dr. Rhea shared the origins of her groundbreaking work. Her book, "The Neo-Agora Chronicles," explored the intertwining of ancient wisdom with modern corporate strategies.

As a young girl growing up in Bangkok, Dubai, and Singapore, with a Greek father and Brazilian mother, her early exposure to diverse cultures eventually gave rise to the renowned business anthropologist of the mid-21st century, Dr. Liana Rhea.

Her eyes lit up with passion, drawing me in as more than just a listener. I was most intrigued by her description of modern businesses as vibrant centers where virtual and physical realms intersected, accelerating the mixing of cultures. "Think of it this way — offices aren't just offices. They're communities, right? How do you see the blend of old rituals and new digital practices playing out with the executives you work with?"

"I've noticed something unexpected actually," I said. "Some people, even much younger than myself, prefer paper and pen. It's like they're balancing on a tightrope between past and future. At a virtual board meeting last week, half were brainstorming on digital whiteboards, while the other half were jotting notes in leather-bound notebooks. It's a fascinating hybrid culture."

Leaning in, Dr. Rhea shared her musings on the new challenges senior executives face, making it feel like a shared concern. "They often wonder about the real benefits of a community-focused culture. What's your take? How is leadership changing to really embrace these ideas?"

Several people came to mind. "It's a mixed bag, really. Some leaders are genuinely transforming," I said, "like a CEO I know who randomly joins video calls to connect with teams — no agenda, just chats. But then you have others who still view 'community' as just another box to check. Last month, one such leader organized a team-building event that felt very forced."

She stared at me with piercing eyes, looking noticeably re-
freshed, which was expected given that it was 7am her time. I wondered if I looked as exhausted as I felt.

A subtle, translucent pop-up floated into my view from the left.
I had forgotten to turn it off. The more I ignored it, the more it
pulsated. So, I glanced at it to make it go away and quickly took in
the words — 'Currently Monitoring: Dr. Liana Rhea, Emotional
Intensity: Moderate, Coach Tip: Dr. Rhea's current neural patterns
indicate she has opened up more than usual. This is an optimal
time to delve deeper into the personal drivers behind her research.'
Ignoring mental pop-ups like junk mail is a skill I haven't mastered
yet.

Dr. Rhea's eyes lit up. "It's fascinating to see how companies
tackle these big questions," she continued. "They're blending old
traditions with new ways of doing things."

She paused for a moment, reflecting further. "Don't you
think some corporate events almost feel like religious rituals? Like
team-building retreats — they remind me of pilgrimages."

"They can feel like that," I said. "Or a company's mission and
values statement. That sometimes feels a bit like scripture."

Here, Dr. Rhea leaned closer, her voice dropping to a more
intimate tone, as if sharing a secret. "Exactly. There is an underlying
connection between ancient traditions and the way we navigate our
professional lives today."

As she spoke, her voice held a wistful tone that hinted at nostalgia. It struck me then — her work was more than academic. Perhaps, it was her way of bridging the vast worlds she'd known: from
the bustling markets of Southeast Asia to the chaotic souks of the
Middle East and the diverse Mediterranean coasts. Her insights
seemed as much a product of her rich upbringing as of her scholarly
pursuits.

I chuckled, "Speaking of blends, I find myself laughing at jokes
in three languages but can't always remember which currency is in
my wallet."

To my right, a nearby avatar detached itself from a group and
approached our table. The figure was nondescript, but there was a
determined look in his eyes.

"Excuse me," the stranger said, "are you Dr. Rhea?"

Dr. Rhea smiled and nodded. "That's me."

The stranger leaned in; his voice laced with disdain. "This whole CorpoCult thing... it's too much. Aren't we losing real connections with all these corporate antics? Aren't you ashamed?"

Before Dr. Rhea could answer, there was a brief flash of light, and the stranger disappeared from the café, replaced by a small notification: "User removed by Café Security."

We both sat in a brief silence, and then Dr. Rhea sighed.

"Does... does that happen often?" I asked.

Dr. Rhea took a moment, her composed demeanor slightly shaken. "Well," she began, letting out a forced chuckle, "as you can see, not everyone likes this topic as much as I do." With a resigned sigh, she leaned back in her chair, the weight of the accusation momentarily clouding her previous vibrancy. Her gaze drifted past me, perhaps seeking solace in the familiar, albeit virtual, landscape of the café. Then, with a wry smile that didn't quite reach her eyes, she returned her focus to the conversation. "Here I am, trying to build real connections, and someone throws 'CorpoCult' at me. Looks like it's back to the grind with spreadsheets and endless PowerPoints."

The buzz in the café resumed, but an unsettled murmur persisted among the patrons.

As I watched Dr. Rhea regain her composure, a thought struck me. What was her personal midlife story? Her passionate pursuit of blending ancient wisdom with modern corporate culture seemed to mirror a deeper, more introspective journey. I wondered if her fascination with creating thriving workplace communities was because of her own search for meaning in this phase of her life.

The signs were all there: the blending of personal history with professional ambition, the yearning for a deeper connection, the reevaluation of one's impact on the world. It seemed Dr. Rhea's journey was not just about redefining corporate cultures but also about her own maturing.

Listening to Dr. Rhea, I noticed her career divided into two phases. Initially, she was driven by a passion for learning, eager to explore cultural traditions and their role in business. This period was all about gathering knowledge and understanding different cultures. However, a shift had occurred, likely spurred by midlife reflection. Dr. Rhea's goals had expanded from merely studying cultures to influencing the corporate world with her insights. There was a determination in her voice to make a real impact, to use her knowledge to drive change rather than just document it. Now, she aimed to craft a lasting legacy, using her experiences to foster more meaningful, connected corporate communities.

Dr. Rhea shook her head slightly, her voice animated with passion. "You know, I don't want to just draft another blueprint to make companies more community focused. I mean, with a bit of AI, anyone could churn that out in no time. I want to go deeper. Why start from zero when we've got centuries of experience to guide us? Instead of always racing to invent something new, maybe we should pause and look back, learn from what's already been tried and tested. We're at this amazing point where the old and the new are colliding. That's the magic I want to explore and capture."

"How can I help you?" I asked.

Dr. Rhea's fingers were lightly tapping the table's surface as she pondered in thought. "I'd love to interview people you think are doing amazing things. Can you think of any? Would you introduce me?"

I nodded. "As you were describing your work, I immediately thought of Joanna in Singapore. Also, Rajiv in Mumbai. And Nicole... I think she's in Paris."

"Ah, yes," she said, "I've been keeping tabs on them. They're making waves. But what about Tomas? The cybersecurity founder from Lisbon?"

I hesitated for a moment, "Tomas, right... After that whole mess with the cybersecurity thing, he's kinda dropped off the radar. Last I heard, he's off the grid. Rumor has it he's on some floating platform off the coast of Portugal. The Nexus Conclave, I believe. It's this sustainable, tech-less community."

She raised an eyebrow in intrigue. "That doesn't sound like him. Maybe there's more to his story." She gave a knowing smile, hinting that she was always one step ahead. Dr. Rhea's dark eyes were filled with excitement.

"You're extremely passionate about this," I said. "Can I ask... why is this so personal?"

She chuckled lightly, "You know, that's a really good question. Growing up, I always felt like I was dipping in and out of different cultures, never really planting my feet in one place. Sometimes I joke that I'm like a one-person multinational company. And that's what's happening in companies these days. They're more like tribes now. So, for me, this research isn't just academic; it's personal. It's about understanding how businesses are remixing the old with the new. That's what I'm really intrigued by – that blend, that special recipe for belonging."

Much like her, I too have always been searching for a place where I can truly feel at home, where the diverse elements of my background can come together. Through understanding how businesses form these close-knit communities, maybe, just maybe, I can understand and craft my own place in the world. This was going to be an exciting project.

After our meeting, I left the cafe, removed my headset, and looked out at the forest below, gently descending toward Byron Bay and the sea in the distance. I was sitting on an elevated porch outside the retreat where I do much of my in-person work. Inside, I could hear the group of senior executives laughing and having drinks after our full day of work. It was time for me to go to bed.

Sands of Synergy

Stepping into the biotech incubator, Dr. Rhea was immediately cooled by a refreshing blast of air conditioning — a welcome relief from Singapore's tropical heat. She took a deep breath, steadying herself for an intriguing day ahead. Today, she would observe how a sand mandala facilitated hyper-transformation among senior executives.

Joanna greeted her warmly. "Dr. Rhea, thank you for coming to observe today's session. Your insights will be invaluable."

Dr. Rhea followed Joanna through a courtyard adorned with lush greenery. "This place," she said, "it's incredible. It feels like an extension of your vision."

Joanna chuckled, "Yes, this is the culmination of years of dreaming and planning."

As they approached the Mandala Room, Joanna explained, "The Sands of Synergy is designed to engage neural pathways that enhance strategic thinking, emotional intelligence, and holistic cognition." She stopped in front of a modern holographic conference decorated like a traditional tearoom, its bamboo mats and porcelain teapots a nod to serenity amid innovation.

Dr. Rhea nodded, intrigued. "So, it's geared towards accelerating cognitive transformation during midlife?"

Joanna nodded. "That's right. But there's also a philosophical layer to it. We're exploring the essence of transformation itself."

"That's what I find so intriguing about your work," Dr. Rhea said. "You're exploring how the brain transitions from resisting to embracing change. What triggers that shift?"

Joanna smiled. "Ah, it's too early to say for sure. I have my favorite idea. But we don't have quite enough data yet."

A large interactive display next to the Mandala Room's entrance flashed faces of various people in the organization. Dr. Rhea noticed a young woman's face among Joanna's 'personal board of directors.' "Your daughter?" she inquired.

Joanna nodded with pride. "She's become an unexpected guide. Taught me to read between the lines, and to see that true healing isn't just about medicine — it's about connection."

Dr. Rhea smiled, reflecting on the stories she'd heard of Joanna's early leadership style — results-driven, no-nonsense.

Joanna led the way into the room. The walls were muted white and displayed minimalistic artworks of serene landscapes and gentle brush strokes. A hint of incense permeated the air. Seven team members gathered silently around a large round table, a colorful mandala at its center. Dr. Rhea's eyes darted across the team, matching the pace of her curiosity.

Joanna introduced Dr. Rhea to Leah Lim — a tall woman with sharp glasses. "Our session facilitator," Joanna said with a smile. "Enjoy observing the session. I'll meet you when it's done."

Leah grinned, "It can get intense. While you're observing, you might get the urge to participate. The mandala has that effect. Feel free."

With a gesture, Leah activated an augmented reality display on the nearby frosted glass wall. A complex mandala diagram emerged, with Humility and Iron Will at its core, encircled by other attributes.

"The exercise blends tech with profound connections," Leah noted. "It's my favorite tool to use in these sessions." Then she raised her voice. "Team. Meet Dr. Rhea. She'll be observing."

Dr. Rhea settled in a discreet corner. The session continued, with the muted shuffle of sand being poured forming a gentle backdrop, almost meditative. Only the individual placing sand would speak. The rest watched silently and were immersed in the moment. Every time a bottle was set down, it signified the end of a personal narrative, allowing the next person to pour sand and share.

As the mandala started taking shape, two team members began a heated discussion over a section of the mandala they both felt passionate about. One believed the sand colors chosen didn't accurately represent the 'Boundless Ideation' trait, viewing them as too avant-garde and disconnected from practical application. The other was a woman with a determined expression who felt that she captured the essence of the trait's innovative spirit. Their voices rose, and the room grew tense.

"These colors you chose," the man said, "they're too abstract, too free-form. We need actionable innovation, not just fanciful ideas."

"Fanciful ideas?" the woman retorted. "You're still missing the point. We need to inspire our people to think outside the box, not just follow the same old patterns."

The man slammed his hand lightly on the table, causing a small quake in the sand patterns. "Innovation is great, but execution matters too."

"We won't make any breakthroughs," the woman shot back, "if we don't take risks!"

Dr. Rhea noticed Leah visibly grappling with the escalating tension. It was a critical juncture. If I was left unresolved, it could jeopardize not just the exercise, but real-world teamwork dynamics.

After a brief silence, another team member who appeared to be a thoughtful-looking man to Leah's right, cleared his throat. "We're looking at this the wrong way," he began. The group suddenly drew their attention to him. "Instead of blending colors, why don't we try a different approach?"

"Such as?" the irritated woman retorted.

The thoughtful-looking man pointed at the mandala. "The 'Boundless Ideation' trait is about cross-functional interaction and learning. Instead of merging colors, what if we use both your choices but in a pattern that shows their interaction and integration?"

The skeptical man raised an eyebrow. "How would that work?"

Leah pulled out a design book and quickly flipped to a page showing a series of intertwining patterns. "Like this. We could use innovative colors in swirls, representing the creative flow. And what might be called practical colors could form the foundation, the core structure from which the swirls emerge. It shows both creativity and grounded execution."

"I appreciate the effort," the woman began, her tone diplomatic yet strained, "but this exercise... it seems like a temporary fix."

"Using swirls and structures doesn't change the fact that we fundamentally disagree," the skeptic interjected. "It's deeper than this mandala."

"This exercise isn't meant to change your views," Leah said. "It's to remind us that despite our differences, we're all working towards a collective mission." She paused, letting her words sink in. "Don't think of this as finding a permanent solution, but rather as a step in understanding each other better."

After a contemplative pause, the woman said, "I'll try, but I can't promise anything."

The skeptic sighed, "I'm willing to go with it for now. But we'll have to address this outside of this exercise."

Leah nodded in acknowledgment. "That's all I ask. Just go with the process for now. Let the experiential nature of the exercise do its thing."

Dr. Rhea observed the interaction closely, noting the unresolved tension but also the willingness to momentarily set it aside for the sake of the team.

The room was thick with intense presence and focus. It was

as if members were pouring their feelings and frustrations into the mandala.

After the resolution, Leah turned to Dr. Rhea and held out a bottle of sand. "Would you care to share your observations with us?"

For a brief moment, Dr. Rhea hesitated, then gracefully accepted the bottle. As she slowly poured the sand, the room waited silently.

"It's evident that there's a deep well of passion here," she began, her voice soft yet confident. "But alongside that passion is hurt, possibly stemming from miscommunication and unmet expectations." She tapped the bottle of sand gently, focused on matching the color lines and curves others had made. "I am... maybe a bit... overcome with the vulnerability you are all displaying by simply engaging in this process. I am struck by your desire to build trust, and your courage."

Her observation, coupled with her genuine demeanor, seemed to resonate with the team deeply. As Dr. Rhea returned to her observer's corner, the atmosphere in the room shifted. There was a renewed sense of purpose and a glimmer of hope.

Almost two hours later when the mandala neared completion, it became evident that the exercise had fostered deeper team cohesion and provided insights into their challenges.

In the lingering silence, Leah rose from her chair. The weight of the moment settled as she gestured toward the mandala. "We've each contributed to this beautiful creation," she began, her voice echoing a sense of finality. "Our thoughts, our challenges, and our aspirations are laid bare in this sand. As in life, change is constant."

With those words, she gently slid her hands into the vibrant expanse of sand, each motion was deliberate, and encouraged others to join her. Their actions were reminiscent of an age-old ritual, and a profound silence enveloped the room. Their hands, intertwined in a dance of unity, swirled the myriad of colors together, erasing the distinct lines and patterns. The once intricately designed mandala became a canvas of blended hues and was a testament to their collective journey.

Beside the table stood a collection of elegantly crafted glass bottles in a neat row. Each was adorned with a delicate label bearing the insignia of the company and the word "Synergy." Leah filled a bottle with mixed sand for each team member. Handing one to Dr. Rhea, Leah said, "For you. A keepsake."

The quiet intensity of the Mandala Room lingered with Dr. Rhea as she stepped out. Joanna was already waiting in the corridor, her silhouette against the play of lights.

"Did the sands of synergy reveal any insights for you?" Joanna's voice broke the quiet.

Holding the keepsake bottle, Dr. Rhea looked thoughtful. "The ending surprised me. It evoked memories of my childhood – the blend of sadness and anticipation when leaving one place for another and starting over."

Joanna began walking, and Dr. Rhea matched her stride. "It's like our corporate culture," Joanna said. "Unique stories but one vision. But... there's something else..."

Dr. Rhea shot a glance at her with intrigue.

"People often label Singapore as a melting pot," Joanna said. "But it's more a mosaic. Every culture shines, yet they form one picture."

"That's the Mandala," Dr. Rhea nodded. "Distinct stories transitioning into a shared narrative. Could this resonate globally, or is it very specific to a place like Singapore?"

Joanna nodded. "I think the Mandala may find relevance everywhere. Modern corporations are more like the mosaic of Singapore than a blended, homogenous culture."

As they reached the lobby, Dr. Rhea observed the juxtaposition of Singapore's modernity and tradition. "Every time I come to Singapore, I'm reminded of the delicate balance between modernity and tradition, between individual identities and a collective ethos."

Joanna smiled, "And that's precisely the Mandala's lesson, isn't it? Recognizing the beauty in diversity and the strength in unity." Joanna's eyes twinkled, "All the tech in the world can't replace genuine connection. That's become the heartbeat of my work."

Dr. Rhea smiled, clutching the sand-filled bottle as a tangible reminder of their shared experience.

A Colorful Festival of Joyful Transitions

Colors soared and laughter echoed across a corporate campus in Mumbai. The inaugural FusionFest was in full swing, taking inspiration from Holi — a Hindu festival deeply rooted in the idea of renewal and rebirth. This age-old tradition, which celebrates spring, love, and new beginnings through the tossing of vibrant colored powders, found a contemporary echo in FusionFest. Amidst this kaleidoscope of joy and chaos, Dr. Rhea, splashed in a myriad of hues, connected with Rajiv Mehta, the CEO of a once-thriving textile factory, now an eco-fashion pioneer.

Shielding his eyes from a splash of pink powder, Rajiv remarked, "You know, moving from synthetic to biodegradable textiles has been exciting. But it's also been quite the journey, grappling with our past and trying to chart a responsible future."

Dr. Rhea detected a hint of defensiveness in Rajiv's voice but couldn't put her finger on it. "I remember the headlines," she said. "The boycott, the backlash. And now, here you are, leading in eco-fashion. Is FusionFest a part of this new chapter for you?"

He paused, sweeping color from his face. "It's our way of hitting the reset button —a symbolic fresh start from past mistakes."

There it was again — a prickliness in his tone. She tried to remember if there had been any previous interactions or disagreements that might have sparked such caution.

The air was filled with a mix of vibrant hues and playful shouts. Meandering through the celebratory crowds, they witnessed impromptu color skirmishes evolve into collaborative brainstorming. As the day progressed, spontaneous teams crystallized, innovative discussions flourished, and the groundwork for a new future was laid. Amidst this vibrant strategy, Dr. Rhea, ever the observer, took copious notes, recognizing the deep cultural wisdom at play.

An unusual gathering caught her eye — a tense semi-circle had formed around two central figures, one a seasoned executive probably in his late forties, the other a younger woman, likely in her early thirties. Their body language was charged with tension — rigid postures, pointed fingers, and raised voices cut through the festive noise. What started as a playful splash of color had spiraled into a heated debate.

Rajiv, spotting the conflict, instinctively moved toward it, then halted, catching himself before stepping in. Dr. Rhea watched, anticipating his intervention.

"Sometimes, it's best to let the storm play out," Rajiv said.

She raised an eyebrow. "But this is FusionFest. Isn't the whole point to foster unity?"

Rajiv nodded, "Unity isn't about suppressing disagreements or conflicts. It's about navigating through them."

Dr. Rhea took Rajiv's cue and watched. She asked, "What is their disagreement about?"

He laughed. "It can be anything. But if I had to guess..." He squinted toward the group, as if he was trying to see the individuals involved. "I'd say it's something to do with the pace of change in the company. She's the only woman in that group."

"I did notice," said Dr. Rhea.

"Anita has real potential," Rajiv said. "I was hoping she would step up today and take the lead. Several of the older men in that group will soon be reporting to her."

Dr. Rhea was impressed with the woman's confidence. "She seems quite dynamic," she said.

"They're airing out their frustrations and resentments. It's cathartic. By tomorrow, they'll have a clearer understanding of each other. And gradually, our middle-aged executives will find a way to adapt."

Dr. Rhea reflected on the faces around her. Each one seemed to mirror the unease of shedding an old identity and the anxiety of stepping into the unknown.

The heated debate eventually turned into a more controlled conversation. Some employees walked away, shaking their heads, while others continued discussing in earnest. It was evident that past rivalries were deep-seated, but the hope was that with time, understanding, and perhaps a few more FusionFests, these differences could be bridged.

As Rajiv and Dr. Rhea wandered through the throngs of celebrating employees, a sudden gust signaled the change in weather. Rain began to fall, gently at first, then with increasing vigor, washing the vibrant powders into swirling rivulets on the ground. Watching the colors blend and disappear, Dr. Rhea was reminded of the mandala's transient beauty from her visit to Singapore, each masterpiece destined to be swept away after careful creation. Watching the colors run together in rivulets on the ground, Dr. Rhea pondered the impermanence of such creations and the enduring impact of the experiences they engendered.

Rajiv, pulling a handkerchief from his pocket to shield his phone from the droplets, glanced at Dr. Rhea with a mix of reflection and concern. "I was quite surprised when I heard you'd be attending today," he confessed as they sought shelter under a canopy. The rain drummed a steady rhythm above them, setting a contemplative tone. "I must admit, I was a bit anxious. FusionFest is close to my heart, and its portrayal matters deeply to me."

Caught off guard, Dr. Rhea responded, "Why would you think I'd be negative about it?"

"I remember a conference from years back," he said. "You spoke about the importance of creating new traditions instead of appropriating them. I guess I've been carrying that memory."

Dr. Rhea smiled, "I've evolved. Over time, I've come to recognize the beauty in blending and adapting traditions."

"So you liked it?"

"I loved it!" She laughed.

The Digital Bonfire in Paris Time

Amidst the shimmering skyline of a virtual corporate world lies a company with a distinct rhythm, resonating with the pulse of the Paris Time Zone. There's no physical building representing it, but its essence is palpable. This unique entity has evolved beyond the traditional confines of employees, suppliers, and clients, creating a boundless global community termed simply as "Collaborators."

Dr. Liana Rhea chose her favorite virtual cafe to meet the company's CEO, Nicole Parker. They chatted before a Digital Bonfire event Nicole would soon be hosting, as a way to prepare Dr. Rhea to participate.

"You've really shaken things up with the brand," Dr. Rhea remarked, a hint of admiration in her voice. "From high-end luxury in New York to cutting-edge tech integration here in Paris."

Nicole smiled wistfully, "It's been quite the adventure. After the luxury market collapsed, we had to reinvent fast. It was really tough, more than I'd expected."

Dr. Rhea asked, "What's been your secret for — what seems on the outside like such a smooth transition?"

Nicole confided, lowering her voice a bit. "One night, it hit me that it wasn't just about skills — it was about letting go of the past." She paused reflectively, lowering her voice and leaning in toward Dr. Rhea. "This might sound strange — but it felt like we were mourning the old ways. That's when I found out about Nostalgia Management. Becoming a certified Nostalgist seemed like the right step."

"That's fascinating. Mourning the old ways? So, what does a Nostalgist do in that context?"

"We find ways to gently steer people away from their comfort in the past, especially now, with the pace of change accelerating."

"I can imagine how that might enhance your role as a CEO."

Nicole nodded. "I've learned to read the team's emotions, to really get where their hesitations come from. It's as much about empathy as it is about strategy."

"A CEO and a Nostalgist, huh? That's quite the combo. Not your everyday executive track!"

Nicole laughed. "I know! I was one of the only business executives in my cohort. Most of my peers were psychologists and life coaches." She paused. "But you know I can't imagine being a CEO without being a Nostalgist."

"Tell me more," Dr. Rhea said.

"Leading through change means understanding how tough it can be on everyone, mentally and physically. If I don't get that, how can I be the leader they need?"

"Wouldn't it be just as effective to have Nostalgists on staff?"

"You would think so. We do have them. But it goes beyond that. When people hold onto memories of what they remember as better, simpler times, my role as a CEO becomes very difficult. I need the tools to help people let go of that yearning."

Dr. Rhea nodded. She wondered if other CEOs would follow in Nicole's footsteps.

Nicole's eyes twinkled as she smiled. "Actually, the Digital Bonfire you're about to see was designed specifically to scale the work of a single Nostalgist."

Moments later, they left the cafe. Dr. Rhea found herself in a forest clearing under a starlit sky with a central bonfire. She sat in a circle with Nicole across from her and Nicole's team spread around the circle.

After a brief meditation, Nicole led the group in 'Future Gazing,' imagining a future where embracing and leveraging constant change had become the norm.

Then the sharing ceremony began. In the virtual glow of a digital torch, each participant took their turn describing the future they imagined while Future Gazing. The torch passed from hand to hand like a blazing talking stick, illuminating each speaker's face with its soft light.

Participants described workplaces that morphed daily to meet new challenges and discussed personal routines enhanced by adaptive technologies. The room buzzed with energy. Each person's vision contributed to a dynamic tapestry that depicted a society thriving on innovation and resilience.

One participant quipped that she imagined the future would feel like a permanent midlife period, constantly reassessing one's identity and sources of self-worth, finding that all of that is deeply intrinsic and has nothing to do with roles and titles. There were nods all around the campfire.

The next person sparked a round of laughter when he quipped, "Who knew a midlife crisis would come in handy like this?"

Really? Because reliving the hormonal rollercoaster of adolescence once wasn't enough excitement for one lifetime? At the same time, she considered whether midlife might actually be a preliminary training ground, a taste of the relentless pace of hyper-change that everyone might eventually navigate. Stripping away the hormone shifts, she thought, permanent midlife-like change might not be all bad after all.

As stories circulated and the warmth of the bonfire was felt,

Dr. Rhea observed one participant becoming increasingly distant. The expressions on his face changed from one of curiosity to deep introspection. With each passing narrative, he seemed to drift away, lost in the powerful emotional undercurrents of the VR experience.

Suddenly, the participant disappeared from the VR space. Another concerned participant remarked, "Did anyone notice where he went? I've seen him do this once before..." And without further explanation, this second participant dropped out as well, presumably to check on the first.

The atmosphere around the bonfire shifted. Hushed conversations ensued. Someone mentioned, "That was Liam. He's been struggling for a while now." Another added, "Yeah, and these VR experiences sometimes become too real. He probably shouldn't have been doing this."

Nicole spoke up. "Liam's reaction is understandable. What he needs is our connection, care, and patience."

After a while, Liam returned to the VR space with a quiet resolve. The participant who had left to check on him whispered words of encouragement.

Nicole gestured to the torch, then to Liam, offering both without a word. Her gesture alone was an invitation — when he was ready, the floor would be his.

The session then unfolded with what Dr. Rhea felt was more vulnerability, and greater understanding.

As the gathering was concluding, an AI narrator crafted a story. Drawing from an extensive repository of folklore and modern tales, it spun a narrative for the future, taking all the sharing that had occurred, and weaving in humor and reflections on shared challenges.

Dr. Rhea reflected on the powerful blend of technology and tradition witnessed at the Digital Bonfire. The synthesis of ancient rituals and modern tools wasn't just effective for business and communication — it seemed to reach into the very core of their human needs, revealing a deep-seated yearning for connection and continuity in a rapidly changing world.

Trust and Transgressions

Dr. Rhea was intrigued by how Rajiv, Nicole, and Joanna had merged traditional practices into their corporate environments, so now she sought out Tomas. She believed that his unique juxtaposition — a tech magnate now immersed in a tech-less realm — could offer profound insights into finding equilibrium in an increasingly digital age.

While waiting to board an early morning shuttle boat, Dr. Rhea looked out over the vast Atlantic Ocean, its waves crashing against the pier, the salt in the air tingling her nose. The Nexus Conclave, off the coast of Portugal, was an hour away. Anticipation weighed on her.

She wasn't sure how to approach Tomas, since she hadn't spoken to him in preparation for her visit. Dr. Rhea had read all the headlines and as many analytical reports as she could find. The facts were clear — following a pivotal advancement in quantum computing that challenged traditional encryption methods, Tomas's cybersecurity firm faced widespread criticism for not anticipating the shift. Top clients experienced significant data, and his firm collapsed. And now he was here, in this remote conclave. What better place could there be to search for purpose in the second half of life?

On the boat ride, with the waves rocking the shuttle, Dr. Rhea took deep breaths, enjoying the sea air. She sat next to an energetic man, who introduced himself as Alex.

"You know, Tomas was a huge part of my life," Alex said. "He was my boss, and my mentor. I owe so much to him."

He now looked vaguely familiar. She sensed admiration, but also a hint of tension. Had she seen him somewhere?

Alex was quite talkative. Dr. Rhea noticed that he looked away, avoiding eye contact as he spoke about Tomas.

"I've achieved so much since I left Tomas's company," he said, rubbing his arm, as if soothing himself. "But there's a gap I can't seem to bridge. I wonder if he ever thinks about the old days as I do."

Alex seemed torn, a man caught between admiration for his mentor and the pain of an unspoken rift. His loyalty was palpable, yet so was the sense of betrayal.

Ahead, the Nexus Conclave emerged, with its platforms sprawled across the ocean like contemporary, eco-friendly islands. Solar panels glistened atop green roofs.

The skipper, an old man with rugged features that could have belonged to a classic film actor — Dr. Rhea pictured Anthony Quinn — enthusiastically pointed towards the Conclave. "They really thought about every detail here," he said. "It's a seamless integration of technology and nature."

He explained how future-proof materials and sophisticated engineering provided stability and sustainability. The skipper announced that the Conclave housed approximately 500 residents, a diverse group consisting of innovators, dreamers, and more than a few spiritual seekers. As they approached, he pointed out the glinting central hub, which shone like a beacon in the morning light, surrounded by residential pods. "Do you see the resemblance to coral polyps?"

She didn't know what to look for, but Alex seemed to get it immediately. Dr. Rhea felt a buzz of excitement as other passengers also murmured in awe, their phones out to capture the breathtaking view.

As Dr. Rhea stepped off the boat, a cool ocean breeze gently tousled her hair. A woman, exuding grace and calm, stepped forward to greet the newcomers. With a soft voice, she introduced herself as Mariana, their liaison.

"Welcome to the Nexus Conclave," Mariana began, "We encourage everyone to unplug and reconnect here, starting by setting aside our digital devices."

Hearing Mariana's words, Dr. Rhea experienced the familiar cocktail of relief, anticipation, and unease that accompanied the start of every detox.

"Tomas isn't here right now," Mariana informed Dr. Rhea.

Dr. Rhea's heart sank. "He's not?" she blurted out, her voice tinged with disappointment. Had she come all this way for nothing?

Alex, catching the change in her tone, added his concern. "What does that mean? Was he on the mainland?"

"He spent the last two days on an island, not far away," Mariana explained. "He'll be back soon."

Dr. Rhea took a deep breath, trying to mask her frustration. She reminded herself to stay open to whatever the journey brought, even if it wasn't what she'd planned.

"Tomas will meet Dr. Rhea in the garden in a couple hours." She looked at her watch. "Maybe earlier."

Dr. Rhea followed the signs to the garden, accompanied by Alex. It was a serene place in the heart of the Conclave, protected from the direct saltwater spray. They walked along a labyrinth path designed for meditation and reflection. Dr. Rhea listened to the leaves rustling in the gentle sea breeze, and the distant murmur of voices. It felt like time was slowing down.

Alex seemed intent on opening up to her. "Since working under Tomas, I've achieved a lot. I started my own tech company, and we're on the verge of something huge. But there's something missing... a voice of conscience, of reason. I want Tomas to be that voice. I'd like to offer him a board position."

Dr. Rhea sensed a hint of desperation in his tone, which she felt came from a deep-seated need for validation and reconciliation. She simply nodded.

"He hasn't answered any of my calls or messages," Alex continued. "So I thought I would come to the man myself."

There was definitely baggage between Alex and Tomas. She wondered now if she had made a mistake inviting Alex to join her in the garden.

"Should I mention I met you?" She asked.

He paused, looking into her eyes. "I'm not sure... Maybe not? I'll... catch up with him later." Then he promptly left.

A few minutes later, the sounds of footsteps approached. Tomas emerged from a side path, his eyes lighting up at the sight of Dr. Rhea.

"Dr. Rhea? I'm Tomas," he greeted with a warm smile, extending a hand.

"Pleasure to finally meet you, Tomas. The Nexus Conclave is even more impressive in person," she remarked, taking in her surroundings.

"It's been a labor of love for all of us here," Tomas replied. As they walked through the garden, Tomas's enthusiasm was evident. He gestured toward a secluded part where a gentle glow emanated from a bioluminescent pool. "Ever seen anything like our Diagnostic Pool?" he asked, his eyes twinkling playfully.

Dr. Rhea stopped, looking intrigued. "The what now?"

Tomas chuckled. "A recent addition," he explained as they approached the pool. "It's like a foot bath, but with insights into your wellbeing. Dip your feet, it's quite enlightening."

As Dr. Rhea tentatively moved closer, Tomas added, "Each color you'll see represents a different aspect of your health."

The pool was framed with smooth stones, and emitted a soft and inviting glow. Dr. Rhea hesitated for a moment. But she was intrigued.

"Care to try?" Tomas asked when he noticed her hesitation. "I find it to be a grounding experience."

Her curiosity piqued; Dr. Rhea nodded. "Alright, why not?"

They both sat by the pool's edge, dipping their feet in. The cool water was soothing. Almost immediately, bioluminescent bacteria responded to the chemical signals from her body, creating a dance of colors around her submerged feet.

Dr. Rhea watched as the glow shifted to a mix of purple with streaks of yellow. Tomas, with a glance at the colors, remarked, "Looks like a hint of high cholesterol and perhaps some dehydration?"

She raised an eyebrow, feigning shock. "High cholesterol? Impossible." Despite her playful tone, she knew he was accurate. Her last health check had indeed indicated a slight uptick in cholesterol levels.

Tomas smiled, leaning back on his hands. "The pool offers insights, not certainties," he said.

She sat in silence, enjoying the sensation of the water and the soft luminescence. The pool, in its simple, understated way, had managed to bridge the gap between them, turning a potentially awkward moment into one of shared understanding and camaraderie.

"It's fascinating," Dr. Rhea murmured, her voice soft and reflective. "These little beings can sense things about us that we can't see — it's both humbling and revealing."

Tomas nodded; his gaze still fixed on the glowing water.

The Nexus Conclave wasn't without its challenges. Tomas opened up about the debates, the occasional rifts in the community over technological advancements. "It's a delicate balance," he mused, "embracing innovation while respecting our core values."

Dr. Rhea listened intently, occasionally interjecting with her own insights. She could feel Tomas's internal struggle, the tug-of-war between his past as a tech innovator and his present as a guardian of ethics.

She looked at her feet and the colours glowing around them. "Yellow is dehydration?"

He nodded.

"I am indeed thirsty," she said. "And, yes, my cholesterol levels are a bit high." She felt a genuine connection with Tomas. "I met someone today who knows you. Alex? I didn't catch his last name."

Tomas's eyes darkened, and he withdrew his feet from the pool. The gentle glow around them dimmed. "Did he send you?" he asked sharply.

Caught off-guard, Dr. Rhea replied, "No, we just happened to share the shuttle. He mentioned you. Seemed... eager to reconnect."

Tomas's expression hardened. "And you know who he is to me?"

She searched his eyes, trying to gauge his feelings. Slowly, realization dawned. Ah, Alex. That Alex.

Tomas looked away; his voice distant. "I have no desire to cross paths with him again."

She nodded because she understood the depth of the wound. Given the history, who could blame him? The pain of betrayal, especially by someone you'd mentored, leaves a lasting mark. "Some wounds are too deep, and don't heal easily," she mumbled.

Tomas sighed, rubbing his temples. With this gesture, she had an intuitive flash. Tomas was here for healing. He said so himself. Was there a part of him that would want to find closure?

Tomas met her eyes again a bit more calmly. "And some bridges, once burned, are hard to rebuild."

Mariana's voice cut through their conversation, "Dr. Rhea? Are you ready?"

Dr. Rhea turned toward Mariana. Ready for what? Then she remembered. Mariana was going to give her a full tour. She jumped up and put her shoes back on.

"You're sitting next to me at dinner," Tomas said, "aren't you?"

"I'd love to. I have so many more questions."

Dr. Rhea followed Mariana, eager to delve deeper into the Conclave's inner workings. They wandered past bulletin boards, each filled with handwritten notes and sketches. Mariana shared tidbits about the community, the collaborative projects, and the organic flow of ideas in the absence of digital distractions.

That evening, under a canopy of twinkling stars, the community came together for dinner. Dr. Rhea was seated next to Tomas, while Alex was at the far end of the table.

As Tomas spoke, the soft glow of candlelight illuminated his face. "Over the years," he said, "every new threat was a reminder of how technology could be turned against us. It changed me. I wore a smile, tried to make light of everything, but behind it, I was always on guard." The shadows danced across his features, enhancing his expressions as if bringing his emotions to the surface. He continued, "Behind every firewall I built, every layer of encryption, was this underlying fear: If technology can be so easily manipulated, what does that say about us, the creators?"

Dr. Rhea, after a thoughtful pause, ventured, "You know, Tomas, from my work with corporate communities, I've observed something. The most resilient and adaptive organizations aren't just built on cutting-edge technology or market strategies. They're rooted in a sense of community, a mutual bond of trust, support, and shared purpose."

Tomas looked intrigued, "Go on."

She continued, "Being here at the Nexus Conclave, it's evident how healing and grounding this community has been for you. I can't help but wonder... If you had built your cybersecurity firm with a similar foundation of community, how differently would things have turned out?"

Tomas let the question sink in. "It's an interesting perspective," he replied.

Near the end of the dinner, newcomers were invited to share

a moment from their lives that led them to seek the Conclave's retreat. It was a tradition that embodied the spirit of the Conclave – a fusion of personal journeys and the collective quest for deeper understanding.

Tomas raised his voice so others could hear, "Dr. Rhea, we'd love to hear about your journey to us. What's the deeper story behind your visit?"

People cheered their encouragement. Tomas smiled at her.

Dr. Rhea hesitated for a moment — a public speaker by profession, she usually felt at ease in front of crowds. But this was an intimate space. She felt like an open book, about to reveal her most private chapter to strangers. She cleared her throat. "I came to meet Tomas," she began, as her voice was wavering slightly.

The air was charged with anticipation as she paused. Encouraging murmurs of "Go on" and nods from around the room urged her to peel back another layer of her story.

Gathering her courage, she continued, "Alright, the real reason I'm here..." The memory of the critic from the virtual café flashed before her eyes. She consciously touched the pendant around her neck, drawing strength from its familiarity. "Not long ago, I was accused of promoting 'CorpoCults'," she pronounced the word with disdain. "An ugly term suggesting corporate entities are mimicking genuine cultural traditions."

There were a few nods of understanding, and Dr. Rhea felt a rush of gratitude towards those who empathized.

"For me," she pressed on, "observing traditions merge with corporations was like... finding a place where my diverse cultural experiences finally came together. Being labeled as a supporter of 'CorpoCults' was like having my life's journey, my identity, invalidated." She took a deep breath, her next words filled with a quiet intensity. "So, what brings me to the Nexus Conclave is this: How do we find, or perhaps more accurately, how do we forge a profound sense of belonging in our work and the communities we help shape?"

The din of appreciation following Dr. Rhea's revelation gradually diminished. As one after another person who had attended the dinner shared their moments, it created a comforting atmosphere of vulnerability and introspection.

More of the attendees shared their tales, and eyes eventually wandered to the far end of the table where Alex was. The animated, confident man from the boat seemed much smaller now, almost shrunken into his seat. The weight of expectation hung heavy on him.

Taking a deep breath, Alex began, "I'm known in the tech world for my work in quantum computing. But behind the accolades and recognition, there's a shadow of choices made, paths not taken, and relationships strained."

He paused, glancing briefly at Tomas, who remained stoic, eyes forward. "Once, I had the privilege to work for a true visionary in the cybersecurity realm. Someone who taught me, guided me. In my ambition, I sometimes overlooked the value of trust, of mutual respect. Choices have consequences, and some choices," his voice shook slightly, "leave a lasting mark."

There was a murmur among the attendees. Dr. Rhea's heartbeats echoed loudly in her ears as she processed Alex's words. She remembered their interaction on the boat, the way Alex's eyes had sparkled with a mix of admiration and regret when speaking about Tomas.

The silence around them was palpable, but beneath it was a current of empathy, of shared human fragility. She stole a glance at Tomas. While she could not read his facial expression, she sensed the churn of emotions beneath the calm façade. The evening had turned into an unexpected crucible of revelations and introspection, and Dr. Rhea felt as much a participant as she was an observer.

Alex took a deep breath, "I came with the hope of finding clarity, perspective, perhaps even a path to mend bridges. I heard that this place, this community, has a way of showing us reflections of ourselves, and I hope to find my own reflection here." With that, he bowed his head, the weight of his words felt in the silence that ensued.

Tomas's expression remained inscrutable, but Dr. Rhea was close enough to see the subtle clench of his jaw, the moisture in his eyes.

As the echoes of chatter and clinking of glasses resumed, Tomas suddenly stood up from the table. "Excuse me," he murmured, his voice quiet but laced with emotion. Without waiting for a reply, he began walking away from the dinner area, headed towards a secluded platform that jutted out into the ocean.

Dr. Rhea felt a tug of responsibility for this and decided to follow Tomas. She paced slowly, giving him a moment to himself. As she approached, she noted the stark silhouette of his figure against the moonlit ocean backdrop. The gentle breeze ruffled his hair, and the sounds of the waves provided a rhythmic undertone to the stillness of the night.

He stood at the very tip of the platform, hands gripping the edge, looking out to the vast horizon. It was as if he was searching for answers in the undulating depths below or perhaps seeking solace in the vastness above.

The sounds of the evening surrounded them — the distant chatter from the dinner table, the soft lapping of the waves against the platform, the intermittent calls of night birds. Dr. Rhea stood silently beside Tomas, her heart heavy with the weight of Alex's words.

She felt a torrent of emotions. Sympathy, certainly, for the raw pain she sensed in Alex. But there was also a surge of frustration. She couldn't help but question the timing of his confession, wondering if it was genuine remorse or a strategically timed revelation to earn him some favor in the community. Yet, seeing Tomas's restrained reaction, she couldn't help but empathize with the depths of betrayal he must've felt.

After a few moments of shared silence, she ventured, "The ocean has always been a place of reflection for me. Its vastness, its depth... it somehow puts things into perspective."

Tomas took a deep, shuddering breath. "I've spent so much time here at the Conclave trying to heal, to find solace. And every time I felt I was making progress; the ghosts of the past would resurface." He glanced in the direction of the dinner table, where Alex was still seated. "Wow. What a... speech."

She couldn't tell if his response was genuine or laced with sarcasm.

He wiped a finger under his eye and nodded. Tomas's voice

dropped to a whisper, his eyes not leaving the dark horizon. "Sometimes, I wonder if part of me wanted out, seeking an escape. Maybe, without even realizing, I paved the way for Alex's actions."

As the two stood there, a sudden gust of wind swept across the platform. Out of the blue, a small flock of flying fish leapt from the water, their silvery bodies catching the moonlight, creating a brief spectacle of shimmering beauty. One misjudged its leap and landed on the deck near them.

Tomas acted swiftly, bending down to scoop up the disoriented fish, holding it gently in his hands. Dr. Rhea noticed the care with which he handled it, even as the fish fluttered and wriggled, trying to escape back to the safety of the water. Without a word, he walked to the edge and released the fish back into the ocean. The fish made a brief leap before disappearing into the dark waters.

Tomas looked thoughtful. "Life is filled with detours, isn't it?"

Dr. Rhea smiled gently, "It looks like that fish managed to find its way back."

"Mm-hm," he said gruffly, with a small smile.

After a moment of silence, Tomas stepped away from the railing. "I'm going to see if Alex is still around."

Dr. Rhea's Epiphany

Traversing the globe and exploring diverse corporate landscapes led Dr. Rhea on a profound inward journey, prompting her to revisit her personal history. She thought about the challenges she faced growing up — never truly belonging, constantly straddling different worlds, adapting like a chameleon to her surroundings. As she immersed herself in stories of corporations reinventing their cultures, she saw a reflection of her own continuous reinvention with each country she called home.

She saw parallels between the blending of team cultures in business and her own experiences of merging cultural identities. Then an epiphany: her adaptability wasn't a void, but a vibrant space of fluidity.

Dr. Rhea's search was not just about the corporations — it was about understanding the universality of the human desire for community and belonging. Her personal quest for identity had led her to a broader realization. Organizations, much like individuals, flourish in a community — particularly those that, like her, embody a spirit of being from both everywhere and nowhere.

This revelation made her understand the paramount importance of leadership traits that fostered such communities.

Fostering a Resilient, Community-Spirited Organization through Midlife Leadership Superpowers

Let's explore how three Midlife Leadership Superpowers strengthen an organization's sense of community: Continual Rebirth, Life Synergy, and Total Ownership. By focusing on these leadership traits, organizations can create a more cohesive and resilient community.

Continual Rebirth: Midlife leaders embodying the superpower of Continual Rebirth leverage their personal journeys of transformation to inspire a culture of continuous learning and adaptation within their teams. By sharing their own stories of evolution, these leaders illustrate that resilience is born from the willingness to embrace change and let go of what no longer serves. This readiness for transformation forms the bedrock of a resilient organization, helping employees perceive change not as a threat, but as a pathway to growth and innovation.

The narrative of Dr. Rhea's journey, exploring the confluence of diverse cultures and traditions, mirrors the organizational process of continual rebirth, where the blending of different perspectives fosters a stronger, more unified community.

Life Synergy: By integrating their personal insights and vulnerabilities into their professional roles, midlife leaders practicing life synergy foster a more human and relatable culture.

Leaders like Nicole, who openly share their transitions and insights, act as role models for a more holistic approach to leadership. This authenticity encourages team members to also bring their full selves to work, fostering a culture of mutual respect, empathy, and understanding.

In this environment, the workplace evolves beyond its conventional limits, transforming into a vibrant community where individuals are valued for their whole selves—not just their professional skills. Dr. Rhea's exploration of communities within corporations highlights how midlife leaders can catalyze a shift towards workplaces that embody the richness and diversity of human experience, creating a more inclusive and supportive community.

Total Ownership: Leaders practicing this superpower cultivate a sense of belonging and commitment among their teams, guiding them to see their work as part of a larger purpose. This sense of collective ownership bolsters the organization's community spirit, with each member understanding their contribution to shared goals.

The transformative power of Total Ownership is evident in the ways midlife leaders like Joanna integrate community-building practices into their business strategies, fostering a sense of unity and purpose that resonates throughout the organization.

Conclusion: Leveraging the Power of Community-Centric Leadership

Dr. Rhea's personal journey, woven through the complexities of being a Third Culture Kid and the modern corporate challenges, brought a compelling revelation: it's not about conforming to predefined boxes but about embracing adaptability, fluidity, and, most crucially, community.

At its core, community — both ancient and in today's corporations — is founded on mutual respect, trust, and a shared purpose.

In today's era of leadership, fostering a sense of belonging is as crucial as providing guidance, ensuring that every individual feels seen, heard, and valued.

Chapter Seven
The Ripple Effect of Mastery

"Legacy is formed by the continuous ripples we create in the lives we touch."

— **Joanna Vega**

CEO Insights at Lake Como

Do you recall that evening by Lake Como where we first met Rajiv, Joanna, Nicole, and Tomas? Amidst the hum of the conference's inaugural cocktail party, our four protagonists found a quiet corner. Bathed in the soft glow of twilight, they exchanged worried glances and shared their apprehensions about the upcoming panel. Caught between the weight of expectations and the truth of their own journeys, they wrestled with a choice: conform to a polished leadership narrative or embrace the raw authenticity of their experiences.

The four friends took their positions on stage as the opening panelists, with the weight of their earlier discussion still lingering in their minds. The theme of this year's global CEO forum hung on a banner behind them — "Bridging Boundaries: Charting the Course of High-Performing Teams." There was a casual elegance in the ambience. White drapes and rich wooden accents adorned the setting. The Italian sun cast its golden glow, making the waters of Lake Como shimmer just beyond the veranda. As the crowd fell silent, all that remained was the soft lapping of the lake against its edges.

The moderator was a gentleman with long, curly silver hair, an elegantly dapper Italian version of Albert Einstein. He quickly introduced each panelist, noting their diverse origins — from Pune to Portugal. Tomas quickly corrected, "From Porto, to be specific," which lightened the mood.

As he transitioned to the next part of the discussion, the moderator reached up and lightly swept back his hair, a gesture that seemed to gather his thoughts as much as it did his tresses. "A mix much like everyone here today." He opened his arm as if taking in all of the participants seated in the small amphitheater. "Could you share how your individual experiences have influenced your approach to 'High-Performing Teams,' as per our theme today?" He looked at Joanna, seated closest to him. "Would you like to start, Joanna?"

"Looking back on the various teams I've worked with," Joanna said, "I've noticed we often did our best when things seemed a bit chaotic. It's kind of like how a piece of complex music uses tension and dissonance to enrich the melody. That same kind of friction in our team didn't just challenge us; it became something we depended on. It drove us to be innovative, to really listen to each other's viewpoints, and in the end, it helped us excel together."

She let the idea hang in the air for a moment, allowing it to resonate with the audience. Then, with a knowing smile that suggested she was all too familiar with the chaotic, yet productive nature of such dynamics, she leaned in slightly, as if sharing a secret. "You know you're in a high-performing team when everyone's arguing passionately, and you can't tell if you're about to split up or win an award for best collaboration."

Tomas leaned forward from his seat at the end of the row of four chairs, so he could speak directly to Joanna. "That sounds like your legacy."

"Oh, nice," the moderator exclaimed. "What do you mean by that, Tomas?"

Tomas addressed the audience. "I get the sense Joanna will leave behind a legacy of love for tension and constructive disagreement. A beautiful legacy, in my opinion."

Joanna smiled at him and nodded. "Sounds right," she said.

The moderator chuckled, "I can already sense today's discussion will be enlightening and, dare I say, entertaining." He turned to Rajiv, sitting to Joanna's left. "How about you, Rajiv? What's your take on 'High-Performing Teams'?"

"High-performing teams," Rajiv began, "embody a collective spirit of ten-out-of-ten commitment. Individual high-performance is nice to have, but deep, shared, collective commitment is a must-have."

Tomas leaned forward. "Just last year, a safety initiative Rajiv pushed for prevented serious accidents. It's not just policies; it's about protecting real lives. It's not about understanding the importance of safety. It's about feeling it."

Joanna added, "It's like finally feeling what others feel, not just understanding it."

"Exactly!" Tomas exclaimed. "That, my friends, is a legacy worth aspiring to."

The audience clapped and the moderator smiled. He turned to

Joanna. "You mentioned a profound shift, from cognitive to emotional empathy. For those new to the concept, it's a deeper form of connection and understanding, isn't it?"

Joanna nodded. "And it develops naturally during midlife, as part of the neurological changes in our brains."

"Interesting points all around," the moderator remarked, shifting comfortably in his chair. "Nicole, what's your take on this?"

"I'm no musician," Nicole started, offering Joanna a warm smile, "but your analogy? It really hit home for me." She paused, reflecting for a moment. "You know, there's this myth we all hear about — the lone genius, the solo superstar. But in reality, especially from what I've seen, high-performing teams shatter that myth every single day."

She shifted in her seat, her smile fading into a more serious expression. "For me, going from being a star player on the soccer field to being part of a star team... it was eye-opening. Humbling, really." Nicole chuckled lightly, almost to herself. "And here's something that might stir the pot a bit: sometimes, the brightest stars among us need to dim their lights a bit, let others shine, for the team to really hit its stride."

She let the idea linger for a moment, glancing around at her fellow panelists and the audience, gauging their reactions. "Sounds backward, right? In a world where everyone's racing to the top, this idea of stepping back can seem... well, counterintuitive. But it's in that very step back—the shift from 'me' to 'we'—that something incredible happens. The team soars. And, in that collective shine, the individual finds themselves glowing brighter than ever before."

Nicole's gaze was earnest, passionate. "It's not about the medals or the trophies. It's about embracing that collective spirit, where together, we achieve something far greater than any one of us could alone. That's where the real victory lies."

Rajiv shifted in his chair, causing it to scrape the floor, and leaned forward to speak. "By dimming our shine, our true brilliance gets the spotlight it deserves."

Nicole smiled. "Is that an Indian saying?"

Rajiv chuckled. "It's what you just said."

The moderator smiled at the camaraderie among the panelists, then he held his finger up, interrupting as politely as possible. "Scusate, everyone, please, just for a moment." He pointed towards the window.

As eyes turned, the room seemed to collectively exhale, momentarily forgetting the weight of the discussion in the face of such natural beauty. The striking canvas of the setting sun painted the sky above the lake in bold strokes of purples, oranges, and deep blues. The colors appeared to shimmer, an ever-changing tapestry that had undoubtedly served as the backdrop to countless such debates over the centuries.

"This," the moderator continued with a gentle smile, "is the soul of our region, a daily masterpiece."

The room lingered in silence, collectively captivated by the view. Then, with a renewed sense of calm and perspective, the conversation gently resumed. "And back to our theme... And you, Tomas, what would you say about high-performing teams?"

Tomas shook his head. "I have nothing to add beyond what my friends have said."

"Oh you must have something to add," said the moderator.

"Actually," Tomas took a breath, and looked at the ceiling. "I don't know." He shook his head, shrugged, and smiled.

"I don't know," Rajiv repeated Tomas's words, smiling.

Nicole chimed in, also smiling, "I don't know either."

The moderator flipped his hair with a puzzled look. "I don't understand."

"OK," Tomas explained. "Here's what I can add. I once thought being a strong leader meant having all the answers. But, when I learned to say, 'I don't know,' the team's dynamic shifted. It created space for them to find the answers. It took away the safety net, so they had to find solutions. High-performing teams thrive on the courage to navigate uncertainty together. For me, this shift has been pivotal. It's a higher level of trust."

The moderator grinned slightly and remarked, "Ironic, isn't it, Tomas? A life dedicated to cybersecurity, a field built on mistrust, and yet here you are, on a journey to trust more."

Tomas nodded, a bit surprised, "You're absolutely right."

The moderator cleared his throat. "As we consider legacies, it's impossible to ignore the inherent challenges that arise. We're all familiar with the concept of legacy systems in IT — outdated infrastructures that become weights and barriers for future innovation. Drawing from that metaphor, how do we ensure our company's legacy enables growth and innovation, rather than limiting it? How do we prevent our present actions and decisions from becoming the 'legacy systems' of leadership? Who would like to answer first? Tomas?"

Tomas nodded thoughtfully. "Great question. Maybe... well, I think you just said, 'actions,' right? Maybe it's less a focus on actions, and more a focus on presence. I like the term, 'Legacy as Presence.' It's an idea that's closer to Executive Presence, than to actions."

The moderator looked puzzled.

Nicole laughed. "Can I try?"

Tomas nodded.

Nicole explained, "Tomas's idea really underscores the significance of our impact through presence. This approach transforms the concept of legacy from a monument of past achievements into a living, breathing, and dynamic force that continuously shapes the future."

Joanna added, "The minute we believe we've figured it all out, that's when we become that outdated system."

Rajiv, with a twinkle in his eye, quipped, "Let's not become the 'rituals without spirit' of leadership. Better to be the spirit that dances through the rules, rather than a beautiful but forgotten ceremony." He winked at Nicole. "Yes, that's an Indian saying. From this one." He pointed at his chest.

Nicole smiled. "Well, if Rajiv's inventing proverbs now, we're definitely setting new standards for legacies!"

The moderator glanced down at his cue cards, flipping through them. "Let's see, what's the final question," he mused aloud. Then, with a cheeky grin, he looked up at the audience, "Non lo so." Seeing a few puzzled faces, he chuckled, "That's Italian for 'I don't know.'" Laughter erupted in the room. Collecting himself, he continued, "Let's open the floor for questions."

A hand shot up from the back, a woman. "I'm curious. What's

one piece of advice you wish you had received when you first became a CEO?"

"Great question," the moderator said. "How about it panelists? In just two or three words, what's the best advice you never got?"

Rajiv leaned into the microphone, his voice calm and deliberate. "Whenever I notice behaviors in my team that I find challenging, I've learned to first pause and reflect on my own actions. How am I, perhaps unknowingly, fostering these behaviors? That would have been useful as a younger CEO."

The moderator smiled at Rajiv. "And in two or three words?"

Rajiv nodded his head, "Reflect before reacting."

Joanna offered a wry smile. "I wouldn't have listened anyway. So no advice from me. Just do you. And learn... learn from that."

Nicole spoke confidently, her message clear. "I wish someone had told me that it's okay not to have all the answers." She looked at the moderator. "Two or three words? It's okay to question."

Tomas shared with a knowing look, "The best advice I never got? Make sure your ego doesn't become the legacy system that needs an upgrade."

The discussion wound down amid the serene landscape of Lake Como at twilight. The attendees began to disperse, and a soft hum of conversation replaced the previously attentive silence. As the crowd thinned, Nicole approached Tomas.

"You seem... contemplative," she said.

Tomas took a moment before replying, his gaze drifting momentarily toward the gentle ripples on the waters. "You know, the moderator's observation about my... contradiction... really struck a chord. Balancing my trust in people with the inherent mistrust in my work... it's been a struggle. I've always been able to compartmentalize, but lately, it's been challenging."

Nicole could sense the depth of his reflection. "Is this about the job or something deeper?"

He sighed, glancing away, then nodded. "Great question."

"You've never seemed cynical to me," she said. "You're always joyful."

He chuckled softly, a melancholic undertone threading through his laughter. "Maybe that's a mask."

"I'm sure that's not true," Nicole said.

Still, the weight of his words hung in the air. As the lingering glow of sunset cast long shadows, one couldn't help but wonder how many of us hide behind masks, and in the dance of life, who truly dances unmasked?

The Swan

In the crystalline waters where the Italian Alps cast their reflections, a revered swan named Alarico swam. Alarico wasn't just known for his immaculate white feathers or his graceful glide; he was revered for his wisdom.

Each year, birds from distant lands visited the lake. They'd come to hear Alarico's tales, stories of eras gone by, lessons learned, and futures yet to be written.

One day, a young egret named Livia approached Alarico with a curious expression. "Why," she asked, "do you always speak of the past and the future, but never the present?"

Alarico, drawing a gentle circle on the water's surface with his beak, replied, "Dear Livia, the past is a mirror reflecting our actions. The future is a canvas, waiting for our touch. But the present? The present is the bridge connecting them."

Seeing Livia's puzzled expression, Alarico continued, "When I recount tales of the past, it's not to dwell in bygone times, but to illuminate our present choices. And when I speak of the future, it's not to dream idly, but to inspire action now."

He gestured towards the majestic villas lining the lake, built by architects of yesteryears. "Their vision is realized today. The stones they set have built legacies. Yet, they began with a choice in a fleeting moment, their present."

Livia pondered this, then asked, "So, our legacy is not about the past or the future?"

Alarico smiled, "Our legacy is indeed about the future, but it's crafted in the present. Every ripple we create today travels outward, shaping tomorrows."

Livia nodded, her eyes reflecting a newfound understanding. From that day, she carried Alarico's wisdom in her heart, understanding that to shape her legacy, she needed to be truly present, making each choice, each ripple count.

From Individual Ripples to Waves of Legacy

Lake Como, with its tranquility and ageless allure, isn't just a silent witness to stories but an embodiment of enduring legacies – where every ripple, be it from a lone swan or a gentle breeze, adds to its tapestry. Drawing parallels, both Alarico's wisdom and the insights from contemporary CEOs unfold the layers of human desire to connect, trust, and to be of value.

Leadership doesn't merely lie in positions or decisions. It resonates in the quiet moments of genuine connections, when trust is cultivated, and in the instances where individuals are made to feel indispensable. It's these individual ripples, these singular moments of influence, that when aligned and amplified, create waves – waves that shape the destiny of an organization and its legacy.

As we delve deeper, let's explore how these individual efforts, when channeled through specific leadership traits, can cultivate a culture that doesn't just celebrate the 'I' but truly embodies the 'We'. A culture where legacy isn't just an aspiration but a collective endeavor.

Fostering a Legacy-building Culture through Midlife Leadership Superpowers

As we close this chapter, we delve into how the Midlife Leadership Superpowers of Timeless Impact, Continual Rebirth, and Humility and Iron Will are pivotal in sculpting a legacy that echoes through generations within an organization. In weaving these superpowers into the fabric of leadership, midlife leaders not only guide their organizations to achieve remarkable milestones but also ensure that the legacy left behind inspires future generations.

Timeless Impact: Leaders wielding the power of Timeless Impact instill a sense of stewardship in their teams, laying the groundwork for a culture that equally prioritizes immediate gain and lasting impact. Their forward-thinking vision simultaneously emphasizes short-term results, long-term value, and sustainability.

The emergence of this trait at midlife often stems from a reflective phase of life, where leaders become acutely aware of their footprint in the world. With years of experience, they understand the delicate balance between achieving current objectives and contributing to a sustainable future. This nuanced perspective allows them to inspire their teams to pursue goals that benefit not just the organization but society at large, thereby ensuring a meaningful and lasting legacy.

Continual Rebirth: The superpower of Continual Rebirth in leadership mirrors the lifecycle of the phoenix, symbolizing renewal and evolution. Leaders who embrace this trait demonstrate that growth and transformation are integral to personal and organizational success. They exemplify that to build a lasting legacy, one must be willing to shed outdated identities and practices and embrace new paradigms.

This adaptability is particularly resonant at midlife, a time when many leaders reflect on their achievements and aspirations. With the wisdom gained from their experiences, they recognize the importance of reinventing themselves and their strategies to stay relevant in a rapidly changing world.

Leadership's commitment to innovation and adaptability becomes contagious, permeating the organization and fostering a culture where continuous improvement is valued and celebrated. It's a leadership style that says, "We honor our past by evolving for the future," encouraging teams to push boundaries and explore new horizons.

Humility and Iron Will: The synthesis of Humility and Iron Will in midlife leaders lays a foundation for a legacy of resilience and collaboration. Humility opens the door to listening and learning from others, facilitating partnerships that enhance the organization's collective intelligence. Meanwhile, the iron will demonstrates a steadfast commitment to the organization's mission, even in the face of adversity. Together, these traits cultivate an environment where team members feel valued and empowered to contribute to the legacy. This balanced approach ensures that the legacy built is not just about the leader but about the collective achievements of the entire organization.

The blend of Humility and Iron Will emerges at midlife as leaders have accumulated enough experiences to appreciate the value of collective success over individual accolades. They learn that true strength lies in vulnerability and the willingness to adapt.

Conclusion: Legacy as an Ongoing Narrative

Drawing from the serene reflections of Lake Como and the insights from modern CEOs, we've journeyed through the realms of leadership and its lasting impact. We've discovered that legacy, far from being a static relic of the past, is a dynamic, living narrative, constantly shaped by our actions and decisions.

Every interaction, gesture of trust, and moment of connection, contributes to this legacy. Each ripple, whether a lone swan's glide or a transformative leadership decision, amasses into a wave that shapes organizational destinies. Your legacy captures both your personal growth and the collective growth of all you influence, expanding far beyond your immediate sphere, echoing through time, industries, and lives.

So, as this chapter draws to a close, remember that reflecting on your legacy serves as a compass, reaffirming your commitment to values, driving you forward, and steering you through challenges.

Chapter Eight
Midlife Rejuvenation and the Next Horizon

"Change, the only constant, offers us the dance floor;
midlife invites us to change the music."

— **Nicole Parker**

Key Insights from Our Journey

As I penned what I thought were the final words of this book, a profound insight emerged, reshaping everything. Throughout these pages, we've journeyed deep into leadership, self-discovery, and midlife mastery. Yet, as I paused and looked back, another theme gradually revealed itself — the transformative essence of midlife rejuvenation. This revelation reshaped my perspective, and enhanced my understanding of leadership and midlife mastery.

I've come to see midlife as potentially a continuous journey of rejuvenation. I revisited the manuscript from this fresh vantage point, culminating in the version you're now reading.

- Chapter One - The Seasoned Executive's New Horizon: This chapter captures a pivotal moment as seasoned executives, gathered by Lake Como, delve into deeper authenticity and connection in their leadership roles, embarking on a rejuvenating journey toward self-discovery and renewed purpose in life's second half.

- Chapter Two - Unfolding the DNA of Leadership Mastery: Here, we follow Nicole's journey, a narrative that illustrates how personal and professional challenges become catalysts for an evolution in leadership and self-renewal. She moves toward deeper introspection, holistic problem-solving, and a richer blend of leadership qualities.

- Chapter Three - Forging Your Executive Presence: This chapter unveils the essence of midlife rejuvenation through Joanna's transformative journey from soloist mastery to orchestrating collective brilliance within her team.

- Chapter Four - Elevating Empowerment to Enterprise-wide Ownership: Through Tomas's evolution from hands-on manager to empathetic, visionary leader, this chapter highlights how midlife rejuvenation empowers leaders to trust and uplift their teams.

- Chapter Five - Lyrical Leadership: Poetry, even if not great, serves as the medium to explore the nuances of wisdom, vulnerability, and the dynamic between assertiveness and introspection, underscoring the rejuvenating power of embracing one's creative and reflective sides in leadership.

- Chapter Six - Transforming Workplaces into Thriving Communities: Looking towards the future, this chapter discusses how leadership can turn corporate cultures into vibrant, purpose-driven communities.
- Chapter Seven - The Ripple Effect of Mastery: We cap off with a look at the enduring impact of intentional leadership actions, showcasing how they can create waves of positive change.

Join me in exploring the journey of midlife rejuvenation, unveiling the joy and potential awaiting every leader poised for change.

From Resilience to Rejuvenation

Early in my coaching career, I often spoke on resilience, driven by questions about leading in an unpredictable world and creating adaptable, risk-taking cultures. Around that time, an Accenture report revealed that 90% of Asian board directors believed their organizations lacked sufficient resilience to handle disruptions — a finding that resonated widely and deepened the urgency of these discussions.

Yet, it felt like something was missing. Resilience suggested to me a relentless battle against adversity — pushing through, managing despite barriers and twists. It was the mindset that had me crossing a rickety bridge blindfolded on a ropes course — which the reader might recall from chapter one — determined to lead rather than follow. While this aptly describes a capacity to bounce back, today's world demands more: it calls for us to thrive amid continuous change.

In my 30s and 40s, resilience was a driving force, helping me push forward through challenges. However, as I entered midlife, the concept began to feel more like a burden. I found myself seeking ways not just to survive but to thrive, even amidst midlife's complexities. Telling myself, "Come on, just get up and go already," became increasingly heavy and exhausting.

At the same time, I was feeling generally happier, more relaxed, and less anxious. Even amid major changes in my life, selling my company, going through a divorce, leaving France. A large body of research shows that people get happier as they age. A U-shaped happiness curve, observed across 145 countries, reveals that happiness dips in midlife but rises again, marking this phase as a crucial opportunity for growth and increased well-being. This evolving understanding of happiness and goals as we age led me to consider insights from leaders in the field of aging and psychology.

Laura Carstensen, professor of psychology and director of the Stanford Center on Longevity, highlights in her TED Talk how aging shifts our priorities. As we grow older, we focus less on trivial concerns and more on what's emotionally important, leading to greater happiness and fulfillment. Her insights suggest that as our perspectives change, we can find deeper joy in our later years. This insight into emotional investment opens up a new perspective: could this shift in priorities foster something more joyful, even rejuvenative, than resilience?

A study by the University of North Carolina — "Happiness Unpacked: Positive Emotions Increase Life Satisfaction by Building Resilience" by Cohn, Fredrickson, et al. — suggests a strong link between daily joy and resilience. By choosing to foster positive emotions regularly, we not only enhance our resilience but also our overall life satisfaction, indicating that joy could be a transformative force in our lives. Could embracing joy be the key to transforming resilience into rejuvenation?

Have you noticed moments in your own life where a shift toward joy has transformed challenges into opportunities? How has this shift manifested in your personal and professional life?

In this phase of my life, the experience of resilience was shifting. It now had less to do with responding to challenges. Instead, there was a sense of leveraging change to create opportunities for growth and joy. The reactive nature of resilience was evolving into a more proactive mindset. And the term increasingly felt like something I didn't need anymore.

From this evolving perspective, I've embraced a broader, more dynamic concept than resilience — Joyful Rejuvenation. It represents a shift towards rediscovering zest and creativity throughout life's changes, focusing on growth and fulfillment. Transcending mere survival to find joy and purpose in continual evolution — how might embracing this concept change your approach to daily challenges and opportunities?

In their journeys, Rajiv, Nicole, Joanna, and Tomas move from resilience to rejuvenation, viewing significant changes as opportunities for profound growth. They demonstrate the liberating effect of letting go of rigid expectations, allowing us to fully engage with the present and connect more deeply with our evolving selves.

- Rajiv transforms safety protocols into an emotional pact with his team, revitalizing his organization's culture.
- Nicole turns a professional setback into a catalyst for team creativity and passion, challenging the notion of constant success.
- Joanna evolves from leading solo to harnessing her team's collective brilliance, embracing the beauty of collaboration.
- Tomas shifts from managing details to leading with vision, creating a culture where every team member contributes to solutions.

As we've seen, midlife can be an exhilarating step towards authenticity. The challenges we encounter are simply the outlines of a new chapter in our lives, one we have the agency to author. By releasing old expectations and welcoming change, we begin to pen a narrative of rejuvenation.

As you reflect on the stories of transformation throughout this book, consider how they resonate with your own journey. What new chapter might you envision for yourself as you embrace the changes of midlife? I invite you to think about what title might best describe the next phase of your life's story.

As we continue navigating our midlife journey, let's reconsider the expectations we've encountered and discover how moving beyond them enriches our midlife experience and beyond. What expectations might you be holding onto that are preventing you from fully embracing joyful rejuvenation?

Navigating the Labyrinth of Expectations

In midlife, we often find ourselves surrounded by a complex web of expectations. These expectations, whether from professional relationships, personal connections, or self-imposed standards, subtly shape our interactions and self-perception.

Professional and Personal Expectations: Imagine waiting for a crucial report at work or contemplating your interactions with loved ones. What do you experience when you imagine loosening the grip of expectation? Anxiety, a sense of impending chaos, relief, or a blend of emotions? This exploration covers both professional scenarios, such as awaiting a senior manager's report, and personal dynamics, like those with a family member. You might notice at times, that letting go, though initially disconcerting, can usher in a sense of curiosity and tranquility.

Reversing Perspectives: How does it feel when others release their expectations of you? It confronted me with feelings of inadequacy and unworthiness, revealing how expectations intertwine bizarrely with perceptions of care, support, and love.

From Expectation to Care: We often conflate expectations with care. This realization was eye-opening for me, challenging the assumption that high expectations equate to deep care. So, how do we maintain care while freeing ourselves from the weight of expectations?

The Liberating Effect of Releasing Expectations: I've found that letting go of expectations can sometimes open doors to new interactions, based more solidly on trust.

Self-Expectations and Personal Growth: Reflect on the impact of shedding your own expectations of yourself. For me, it raised fears of complacency and mediocrity. But what if releasing these self-imposed standards actually leads to liberation and a truer sense of self?

Aspirational Mindsets Over Expectations: Transitioning from detailed expectations to broader aspirations can redefine our approach to achieving outcomes and fostering relationships. Embracing a vision of boundless potential encourages us to see and acknowledge the intrinsic worth in ourselves and others.

Transformation in Midlife Through Aspirations: Adopting an aspirational mindset opens us to rejuvenation and a deeper understanding of our evolving purpose, encouraging us to craft a narrative that honors our past and future.

Midlife offers an opportunity to rewrite our narrative, actively shaping a fulfilling future.

Looking Ahead: Life at 100

In an age where our lifespans are longer than ever, contemplating our lives at 100 can yield benefits for the present and future. For example:

- Reinvigoration of Career — Inject new energy into your professional path by rediscovering purpose and passion.
- Enhanced Self-awareness — Gain clarity on your core values and aspirations.
- Long-term Strategic Vision — Think beyond the immediate to consider legacies spanning generations.
- Personal and Professional Alignment — Ensure your actions reflect your values, merging personal passions with professional ambitions.
- Authentic Leadership — Develop a leadership style rooted in genuine self-understanding.

Several years ago, a bulletin board outside a primary school classroom caught my eye, just as I was about to walk into a parent-teacher meeting. The block letter title on the board posed a question, "Who will you be at 100?" Below, kids had scribbled their answers on colourful stickers. "When I am 100 years old, I will be an old lady," read one. "I will still be a singer," pledged another. Other proclamations ranged from a somber "I will probably be dead," to an optimistic "When I am 100 years old, I will be alive."

The traditional career arc – forty years of work, retiring at sixty-five – is gone for most of us. This invites a redefinition of your professional and personal trajectory, and a chance to reassess your foundational values and their role in guiding your leadership. The possibility of spending thirty or even forty years beyond the traditional retirement age has profound implications, challenging us to envision a future far beyond immediate business cycles, one threaded with our deepest ambitions.

Envisioning your life at 100 isn't fortune-telling but a journey of self-discovery, inviting introspection and realization to cultivate a more authentic leadership style.

It encourages reflection: are my actions aligned with my core values? If the answer is 'no', it's an opportunity to pivot and realign your leadership approach. This introspection enhances your leadership's authenticity and effectiveness.

A Visioning Exercise

Whether you find clarity in quiet moments of reflection, during a run, or in the calm of a long shower, these practices can serve as gateways to insights about your personal and professional journey. The purpose here isn't just to encourage action but to highlight how simply engaging in this exercise can subtly shift your perspective on the longevity of your professional life, inviting you to explore various paths to uncovering your leadership potential and life aspirations.

Imagine you're at a significant milestone in the future — whether that's 100 years old or another age that feels significant to you. Think about who's with you, where you are, and what brings you joy. This exercise isn't about crafting a perfect scenario but about exploring the values and connections that give your life meaning. Engaging in this contemplation can itself initiate a transformation, gently expanding your view of what's possible in your professional journey. It's okay if you can't visualize specifics; sometimes, just pondering these questions can open new avenues for growth and fulfillment.

Envision yourself sharing your experiences and passions with others, whether that's on a stage, in a community meeting, or through a blog. What messages do you most want to share? This moment of sharing doesn't have to be grandiose; it's more about the internal realization of your enduring impact and the legacy you wish to leave. By imagining these future interactions, you naturally start to shift towards a mindset that sees a longer, more varied professional life as not only possible but desirable.

Reflecting on your future self can be enlightening, but remember, this reflective journey itself is valuable, subtly guiding you to redefine success in terms that resonate deeply with you, possibly envisioning a broader definition of impact and fulfillment that spans a longer timeframe than you'd previously imagined. If you have trouble imagining anything, don't worry — simply reflecting on who you will be decades from now can shift your perspective.

It took me time to realize the transformative power of simply engaging in this visioning process. One evening, after dinner, I went for a walk to reflect on the question. My thoughts drifted to my grandmother, whose life spanned incredible changes and challenges. She was a toddler during the First World War, a young adult during the Second, and a bit older than me when Armstrong walked on the moon. She had lived through the Great Depression, homesteaded in Texas and New Mexico, flown on jets all over the world, ridden a camel in Jordan, walked along the Great Wall of China, visited Moscow before the Berlin Wall came down, and spent several summers at my home in France.

This reflection made me appreciate not just the tangible outcomes of such an exercise but the profound internal shifts it can inspire, nurturing resilience, joy, and adaptability within me.

On my walk, as I listened to the nighttime symphony of nature, I contemplated the broader implications of envisioning my own future. This wasn't just about setting goals; it was about opening myself up to a future filled with potential, well beyond traditional expectations of professional life.

I saw myself at sunrise, on a wooden balcony, looking out over a forest toward the sea in the distance, with a cup of coffee. I was at an offsite retreat, where I was about to start doing my work. The image felt very much like mornings of retreats I already run, today, coaching C-suite teams. But there was something different.

A handful of people were at the retreat and would soon be waking up. I was about to facilitate a workshop for a group of CEOs and other heads of organisations. What most surprised me was the presence of people that seemed to be heads of religious organisations. But that wasn't quite it — I knew that they weren't church leaders or religious in the sense we generally understand. They were senior executives of future versions of today's large corporations, new types of organisations focused on the well-being of all stakeholders, and whose employees were drawn together by a common connection and a strong sense of community.

As you ponder who you'll be in the years ahead, let the act of envisioning guide you. This process, subtle yet powerful, can unveil new dimensions of your career and life, encouraging a longer, richer professional journey than you might have considered.

Many of us dream of reaching milestones several decades away. Yet, for others, peering just beyond the immediate horizon is a significant challenge. Enter Azman, whose story illustrates that sometimes, even without a clear vision of the future, simply questioning and exploring our present boundaries can gradually open us to broader possibilities.

Transcending Fate

Azman, a 43-year-old Chief Development Officer at an energy conglomerate, wanted to improve his health, yet he quickly set boundaries: "Just don't ask me to quit smoking," he declared at our first meeting, immediately taking that option off the table. Azman's physique suggested a lack of activity, and he confessed to having evaded medical check-ups for nearly a decade.

During a particularly reflective session, Azman expressed a rather ironic sentiment that illustrated his internal struggle. "I'd be furious if I caught my son smoking," he said, smelling of fresh cigarette smoke from his break before our session. This contradiction highlighted his awareness of the damage his habits were causing, yet his strong instinct to protect his son from similar harm.

When prompted about his long-term goals personal, he struggled to envision anything beyond the immediate future. Which was also ironic, given that in his professional role, Azman would typically be engaged in long-term strategic planning due to the nature of the industry, which involves substantial investments, long project timelines, and regulatory considerations.

"You're skilled at strategic planning in your professional role," I said, "projecting decades into the future. What if you looked at your life as a project you need to plan long-term for?"

Azman leaned forward slightly. "That's an interesting angle." He paused, his brow furrowed. "But honestly, it doesn't seem possible to think so far ahead personally. In my job, sure, we plan decades ahead, but life... it's not the same, right? There are no guarantees." He smiled, catching what he had just said. "Of course, no guarantees in business either."

"Putting the uncertainty aside," I said, "if you were to imagine it's decades from now — what would you hope to see?"

Azman sighed, crossed his arms, and stared past me, focusing on something invisible in the distance, as if trying to picture his future on the blank wall before him.

A shadow crossed his face. "Look, I'm destined to die at 50, just like the other men in my family. It's in my genes," he muttered, his voice a mixture of resignation and defiance. The thought seemed to drain him, his shoulders sagging under the burden of inevitability. "How can you plan for ten or twenty years when you can't even see tomorrow?" he asked, his tone laced with a deep, almost palpable dread of his perceived fate.

Yet, he dared to pose the question to himself — "Who will I be decades from now?" This in itself was a significant shift. Though his immediate, intellectual answer was dismissive — "I'm destined to die at 50" — I am convinced that the very act of asking this question had begun to resonate within the depths of his subconscious, subtly stirring currents of change.

Our conversation turned to epigenetics, as I explained how our environment and daily choices can actually 'talk' to our genes, potentially altering their expression.

Azman's brow furrowed as he absorbed this. "So, you're saying that my decisions could rewrite some of my genetic destiny?" he asked, a spark of curiosity igniting in his eyes. This new understanding seemed to empower him, offering a sliver of control over the fears that had long governed him.

As we chatted, I learned his wife was a doctor, which added another layer to our dialogue. Reflecting on his earlier comment about his son, I wondered how his wife must feel, watching him compromise his health. Further inquiry into his family history uncovered that not all male relatives passed away before 50, a fact that Azman related with surprise, as if recalling something he had forgotten.

His guarded demeanor softened, replaced by a tentative openness to reconsider his own future. "Maybe I've been too quick to accept my father's path as my own," he murmured, the realization beginning to dismantle some of the walls he had built around his expectations of life.

Gradually, Azman began to dream bigger, expressing hopes of being present for his youngest daughter's significant life events — her graduation, wedding, and the birth of her children. He was able to imagine these future events. This vision extended far beyond a mere five-year outlook; he was now imagining his life two decades ahead.

Challenging our self-imposed limits requires courage, persistence, and a rigorous self-examination. Often, it's a path we choose only when we feel we have no other options, especially when our identity, relationships, and the legacy we wish to leave behind are on the line.

Yet, embarking on such journeys can lead to extraordinary outcomes. Azman's dedication to changing his life's trajectory was validated when a thorough medical exam revealed his health was largely manageable, requiring only minor adjustments.

Translating Long-Term Insights into Immediate Presence

Let's explore some of the key benefits we've highlighted from the start of our future visioning journey.

Reinvigorating Your Career:

Many executives feel a sense of stagnation after years of success, wondering, "Is this all there is?" This sense of an endpoint can dampen the drive to explore or take risks, making your perspective narrow. The mind becomes clenched, focused on missed opportunities, dwelling on past decisions, and wondering if different paths taken earlier might have led to greater satisfaction or achievement.

An executive I worked with once said, "I'm just coasting, waiting for retirement." This feeling reflects a mindset that professional life ends pretty much at 65.

However, reflecting on the wisdom and experiences of your centenarian self changes this view entirely. Suddenly, 65 becomes just another milestone, not an endpoint. This perspective rekindles your passion and opens up new possibilities, turning challenges into opportunities for growth.

Enhancing Self-awareness:

Seeing your productive years as limited can narrow your focus to the immediate, making every decision feel critical. But envisioning a longer future broadens your perspective, allowing for clearer decision-making and aligning your actions with a more meaningful legacy.

However, when you stretch your perspective, visualizing additional decades of productive years ahead, your understanding of the present moment evolves. The "here and now" expands.

A CEO realized she had been viewing younger professionals as potential successors to groom. With a broader outlook, she began to see them as partners, enriching cross-generational collaboration.

Long-term Strategic Vision:

A short-term focus might make quick wins appealing, but envisioning a longer future shifts your strategy. You start playing the long game, considering how each decision contributes to your legacy.

A CTO realized that she had become hesitant to embrace new technologies, and that this might have been rooted in a belief that she wouldn't be around to witness their full impact or tackle their challenges. With a renewed perspective, she felt more inclined to champion innovation, knowing she'd be guiding its integration for years to come.

Personal and Professional Alignment:

Previously, you might prioritize work over significant personal moments. Viewing your life through the lens of a centenarian, you realize the importance of balancing these aspects, making decisions that enrich both your personal and professional life.

I once coached a CFO who spent the majority of his time overseas, away from his family. As the date of his daughter's high school graduation approached, he said to me, "Soon she will be off to college and I will never have her at home again. This whole period of life is coming to an end. And I'm not there." The overwhelming sense of impending loss was clouding his professional judgment, turning into resentment towards his colleagues, as if he felt like he was wasting time with them when he should have been home with his daughter. By expanding his gaze, he shifted from feeling loss to recognizing potential. He envisioned shared journeys and mentorship opportunities with his daughter. This fresh outlook not only rekindled their bond but also clarified his professional vision.

Authentic Leadership:

With a short-term view, leadership can become about meeting external expectations. But aligning with the values of your envisioned elder self fosters a leadership style rooted in authenticity, deeply connecting with others and building trust.

These insights invite you to stretch the canvas of your potential, guiding your leadership with the wisdom of an extended future. This approach not only commands respect but fosters genuine connections and a shared mission.

Fostering Joyful Rejuvenation through Midlife Leadership Superpowers

We've looked at Midlife Leadership Superpowers through various lenses, including executive presence, enterprise-wide ownership, and change and reinvention. Now, let's focus on how these powers can rejuvenate your midlife journey, leveraging Life Synergy, Continual Rebirth, and Boundless Ideation.

Life Synergy: By midlife, many leaders have developed ways to merge personal passions and professional roles. This convergence of personal and professional life acts as a catalyst for rejuvenation, infusing work with deeper meaning and passion. Life Synergy transcends traditional work-life balance by merging these aspects into a fulfilling whole.

Continual Rebirth: This is like a fountain of youth, allowing leaders to continuously evolve and reinvent themselves. There's a zestful excitement in shedding old labels and trying on new identities, like an actor exploring different roles. This superpower flourishes in midlife as the accumulation of experiences provides the wisdom to recognize the impermanence of roles and the courage to explore new facets of oneself.

Boundless Ideation: As we've seen, midlife can unlock creativity, turning problem-solving into a dynamic and innovative process that refreshes your professional approach and inspires your team. Like a second spring of the imagination, rejuvenating your approach to challenges and invigorating your team and organization with a culture of vibrant possibility.

On the Cusp of Your Next Chapter

As we draw this book to a close, I'm struck by a sort of symmetry, as I reflect on the unexpected turn this final chapter took — revealing the profound affection I have for the midlife journeys of so many people I have coached, prompting me to re-write this book. We seem to always be perched at the edge of a new discovery, a new twist, a re-write, those aha-moments that add richness to our story.

The end of a book, much like reaching midlife, isn't a conclusion. It's more of a gateway; an open door to new beginnings, fresh insights, and limitless possibilities. Just as this book morphed into something more than I initially thought, so too does our current stage in life. The experiences we've gathered, the wisdom we've soaked in, and the lessons we've learned – they're all setting the stage for what's next.

Here's to the unwritten pages of your story, the uncharted territories of your journey, and the boundless skies of your future adventures. Cheers.